1890 UNION VETERANS CENSUS

Special Enumeration Schedules
Enumerating Union Veterans
and Widows of the
Civil War

Missouri Counties: Bollinger, Butler, Cape Girardeau, Carter, Dunklin, Iron, Madison, Mississippi, New Madrid, Oregon, Pemiscot, Petty, Reynolds, Ripley, St. Francois, St. Genevieve, Scott, Shannon, Stoddard, Washington, and Wayne

Transcribed and Compiled by
Linda L. Green

WILLOW BEND BOOKS
2012

WILLOW BEND BOOKS
AN IMPRINT OF HERITAGE BOOKS, INC.

Books, CDs, and more—Worldwide

For our listing of thousands of titles see our website
at
www.HeritageBooks.com

Published 2012 by
HERITAGE BOOKS, INC.
Publishing Division
100 Railroad Ave. #104
Westminster, Maryland 21157

Copyright © 1999 Linda L. Green

All rights reserved. No part of this book may be reproduced or transmitted in any form or by any means, electronic or mechanical, including photocopying, recording or by any information storage and retrieval system without written permission from the author, except for the inclusion of brief quotations in a review.

International Standard Book Numbers
Paperbound: 978-0-7884-3159-3
Clothbound: 978-0-7884-9333-1

Table of Contents

County	Page
Bollinger	1
Butler	8
Cape Girardeau	13
Carter	23
Dunklin	26
Iron	32
Madison	36
Mississippi	40
New Madrid	44
Oregon	46
Pemiscot	50
Perry	52
Reynolds	57
Ripley	59
St. Francois	62
St. Genevieve	67
Scott	70
Shannon	74
Stoddard	77
Washington	83
Wayne	88

BOLLINGER CO. MISSOURI
SPECIAL ENUMERATION 1890
UNION VETERANS CENSUS
Microfilm Number M123-28

Eleventh US Census 1890 Schedules Enumerating Union Veterans and Widows of Union Veterans of the Civil War. MISSOURI Roll 28 Bundle 88 includes the following Missouri Counties: Bollinger, Butler, Cape Girardeau, Carter, Dunklin, Iron, Madison, Mississippi, New Madrid, Oregon, Pemiscot, Perry, Reynolds, Ripley, St. Francois, St. Genevieve, Scott, Shannon, Stoddard, Washington, and Wayne

Names are arranged in order of appearance and are not alphabetical. Standard abbreviations for this county include: MO for Missouri, IN for Indiana, ILL for Illinois, Cav for Cavalry, Col for Colored, Inf for Infantry, Lt for Light, Arty for artillery, BN for battalion, PA for Pennsylvania, Res for reserve, Vet for veteran, MSM for Missouri State Militia, TN for Tennessee, Kan for Kansas, Vol for volunteer, NY for New York, KY for Kentucky, Mtd for mounted, Ark for Arkansas, OH for Ohio.

NAME/UNIT/DATES SERVED
Union Township

Dennis, George W.--29MO Inf, Aug1862-17July1865
Slinkard, Henry--47MO Inf,06Aug1864-29Mar 1865
Slinkard, William A.--3MO Cav,Nov1863-14July1865
Ragsdal, Anthony--47MO Inf,27Aug1864-29Mar1865
Dollar, Milus--50MO Inf,31Aug1864-21Mar 1865
Holbrook, Jefferson--5MO Cav,30Mar1862-14Apr1864
Carlton, Edward--32ILL Inf,31Aug1861-15Sep 1864
Skaggs, James--50MO Inf,22Sep1864-08Apr 1865
Edmonds, James T.--50MO Inf,Sept1864- Apr 1865
Smith, George W.--47MO Inf,30Aug1864-29Mar1865, widow--Isabel
Keiser, Henry--8MO Inf,15Aug1861-07July1864, widow--Rachel
Burcham, Joseph A.--32ILL Inf,01Oct1861-30Oct1864
Smith, A. H.--9MO Cav,24Feb1864-08June1865
Myers, Isaac--47MO Inf,15Aug1864--29Mar1865
Book, William F.--50MO Inf,15Sep1864--11Apr1865
Hahn, Abraham--47MO Inf,1Sep1864--29Mar1865
Mason, Henry--47MO Inf,20Aug1864--29Mar1865
Adams, David--47MO Inf,01Sep1864--29Mar1865
Holbrook, Francis M.--47MO Inf,15Aug1864--29Mar1865,widow--Mary
Hirtman, William--47MO Inf,15Aug1864--29Mar1865
Steakley, James C.--1Ranger BN,8Aug1861--12Dec1861;12MSM Cav,12Dec1861--23Oct1865
Nations, James W.--5MO Cav, 12Mar1862--14Apr1864; 47MO Inf 20Aug1864--29Mar1865
Brites, George W.--2MO Arty. 25Feb1864--24Aug1865
Long, Andrew J.--47MO Inf,01Sep1864--29Mar1865
Smith, Henry J.--3 MO Cav,15Feb1864--12Jul1865
Knowles, James M.--11MO Cav,27Feb1864--12Aug1865
OKelley, Thomas K.--2Ark Cav,23Mar1864--28Aug1865
Conrad, John C.--5MO Cav,13Mar1862--28Mar1864;13MO Cav,29Mar1864--13May1866
Johnson, Marion--3MSM Cav,03Aug1863--13Jul1865
Yount, Franklin--3MSM Cav,14Feb1864--13Jul1865
Deweas, William--5ILL Cav, widow--Dolly
Grindstaff, Jacob--47MO Inf,01Sep1864--29Mar1865
Grindstaff, Peter--47MO Inf,01Sep1864--29Mar1865, widow--Rebecca

Johnson, James--50MO Inf,01Feb1865--11Apr1865, widow--Margarett
Martin, Calvin--12MO Cav,25Jan1864--17Apr1866
Robinson, Joseph--2MO Arty. 10Jan1864--24Aug1865
Hicks, Joseph--11MO Inf,21Sep1864--02Nov1865
Smith, Ransom J.--47MO Inf,01Sep1864--09Apr1865; former widow—Rebeccca
Sefler, Robert L.--7MO Cav,09 Sep1863-17Jul1865--Alias Robert Lee
Dollum, Lucinda C. Widow
Heartle, Mary L. J. Widow
William, Charles US Soldier
Gibbs, James P. US Soldier
Jones, Francis M. US Soldier

Whitewater Township

Barber, Samuel C.--2ResCorpVet,10Aug1861-07Sep1864
Hartle, Henry S.--3MO Inf,28Jul1863-07Jul1865
Statler, Aaron--32MO Inf,18Feb1865-18Jul1865
Masters, John C.--2MO L.Arty 25Feb1864-24Aug1865
Statler, Alvin J.--47MO Inf,Aug1864-29Mar1865
Statler, Peter--30MO Inf,30Sep1864-23Apr1865
Conrad, William--50MO Inf,15Sep1864-11Apr1865
Hartle, Bennett P.--50MO Inf,15Sep1864-11Apr1865
Murray, Henry J.--5MO Cav,26Sep1863-08Jul1865
Jaco, Thomas--5MO Cav,14Mar1862-25Jul1865
Propest, David--50MO Inf,23Sep1864-11Apr1865
Conrad, Alfred--5MO Cav,13Mar1862-25Mar1865
Statler, Conrad--50MO Inf,22Sep1864-11Apr1865
Barks, Conrad--30MO Inf,20Oct1864-23Apr1865
Clay, Henry--50MO Inf,03Sep1864-11Apr1865
Crites, Solomon--2MO L.Arty 25Feb1864-24Aug1865
Shainch, Nicholas--5MO Cav,13Mar1862-25Mar1865
Gardner, M. W.--30MO Inf,01Oct1862-21Aug1865--widow Salina H.
Shrum, Frederick--30MO Cav,28Jul1863-13Jul1865
Conrad, Joseph S.--47MO Inf,15Aug1864-29Mar1865--widow Francis E.

Conrad, Peter R.--1MO Inf,20Sep1861-30Sep1864
Johnson, Abraham--12MO Cav,07May1862-07May1865
Conrad, Francis M.--50MO Inf,12Nov1861-01Mar1864;52IND Inf,02Mar1864-07Sep1865
Books, John F.--5MO Cav,18Jul1863-08Jul1865
Wills, William--13MO Cav,Apr1862---Mar1865
Leonard, Henry A.--10MO Cav,09Sep1862-22May1865
Garner, Samuel--50MO Inf,22Sep1864-11Apr1865
Statler, Littleton L.--50MO Inf,22Sep1864-11Apr1865
Miller, Elihu L.--2MO Cav,05Sep1862-04Sep1865--widow Elizabeth
Nations, George B.--47MO Inf,15Aug1864-04Sep1865
Schlatiz, Frederick O.--Soldier
Burke, Jr., Daniel--Soldier
Frize, Christian--Soldier
Lobringer, August--Soldier

Crooked Creek Township

Green, James--83Kan,1863-12Dec1866
Leming, James B.--30Ill Inf,20Aug1861-13Jun1862
Reagan, Richard R.--50MO Inf,03Sep1864-08Apr1865
Segrumer, John—Confederate Cav,08Aug1861-26May1863
Reagan, James G.--5MO,27Jul1863-08Jul1864
Mattes, Henry L.--50MO Inf,31Aug1864-21May1865
Panielt, William D.--4MO Inf,11Oct1861-01Mar1862
Stady, Christian J.--13MO,13May1863-28Mar1864;5MO Cav,09Dec1861-20Dec1863
Jenkins, George W.--8TN,22Nov1864-01Aug1865
Robin, Monrow--47IND Vol,06Aug1864-28Mar1865
Arthur, Joseph--5OHIO Cav,16Sep1861-20Dec1864
Balton, John P.--Soldier US

The following show up in this township but lived in Madison Co. MO:
Morris, Louis W.--80OHIO Inf, 21Aug1862-26Aug1863
Slinkard, Peter--5MO Inf,16Jul1864-18Jun1865
They have been added to the Madison County MO1890 census.

German Township

Williams, Marshal H.--69MO Cav,23Mar1865-18Jul1865
Mayfield, Albert E.--widow Jullie A.
James, John W.--Pvt.
Stattler, Adam J.--50MO Inf,15Mar1864-15Sep1865
Stattler, John C.--56MO Cav,07Aug1762-01Dec1864
Fiknart, Henry--2MO Cav,Jul1864-22Feb1865
Jones, Moses--81ILL Inf,19Dec1863-31Jun1865
Masters, Elisha--8MO,May1865-08Nov1865
Stattler, Jesse--8MO,May1865-08Nov1865
Jordan, John M.--Served 1 Month—No Unit Given
Yount, John S.--69MO Cav,23Mar1865---Jul1865
Laupher, Benjamin F.--MO.Militia,1862-1864
Slinkard, James E.--2MO Cav,1864-served 3 months
Killian, Phillip--2MO Cav,1863-served 1mo.15day
Green, Alford C.--24MO Inf,1861-served 10 months
Self, Joseph R.--50MO Inf,03Sep1864---Jun1865
Purch, Thomas A.--47MO Cav,Mar1862---Jun1865
Williams, Elvis,78MO Cav,26Sep1864-26Feb1865
Mayfield, John J.--MO Cav,Apr1861------1864
James, Henry--79MO Cav,Apr1863---Mar1865
James, Ransom L.—No Unit Given,07Mar1865-07Jul1865
James, James P.--69MO Cav,23Mar1865-3mo.15day
Patton, William D.--2MO L.Arty 15Feb1864-25Dec1865
Lincoln, Jacob M.--5ILL Cav,17Sep1861-21Jun1862
Barks, Jesse T.--81Ill Inf,12Aug1862-17Jul1865
Schrock, Berthold—No Unit Given,Aug1861---Sep1861
Estes, John F.--69MO Cav,23Mar1865-19Jul1865
Cole, John J.--79MO Cav,Apr1865-03Jul1865
Norvel, David M.--69MO Cav,23Mar1865---Jul1865
Pierce, Alexandra--47MO Inf,Sep1864-31Mar1865
Seabaugh, Francis E.--50MO Inf,03Sep1864-29Jun1865
Estes, James K.--69MO Cav,23Mar1865-18Jul1865,widow--Hanah A.

Chostner, James M.--79 MO Cav,26Aug1864-26Feb1865
Seabaugh,Christopher--27ILL Inf,11Jun1861-03Apr1862

Lorance Township

Crader, Jonus H.--6MOVolCav, 13Aug1864-13Nov1865
Chandler, Josephus--6MOVolCav, 01Sep1864-13Nov1865
Stoval, Asa--56MO Cav,01Sep1864-09Dec1864
Bullock, John H.--31ILL Inf,12Aug1863-10Jul1864
Kinder, Mathew--2MO Cav,13Mar1864-25Aug1865
Lusley, John H.--6MOVolCav,13Aug1864-13Mar1865
Shanks, Soloman--6MOVolCav,13Aug1864-13Mar1865
Fox, James H.--2MO L.Arty, 03Jun1863-24Aug1865
Allen, James W.--6MOVolCav, 13Aug1864-13Mar1865
Hahs, Daniel--6MOVolCav, 10Jul1864-10Mar1865
Brown, L. C.--6MOVolCav, 13Aug1864-13Mar1865
Buchanan, William T.--MO VolCav, 13Mar1862-29Mar1864
Leaver, George--5TN Cav,10Aug1862-29Oct1863,widow-Marg
Coites, Joab--6MOVolCav,13Aug1864-13Mar1865
Dachius, John K.--6MOVolCav,13Aug1864-13Mar1865
Aldrich, Isaac M.--2MO Cav,10Jan1863-24Aug1865
Newel, Terril H.--6MOVolCav, 13Aug1864-13Mar1865
Banks, George--6MOVolCav,13Aug1864-13Mar1865
Bowman, B. S.--2MO L.Arty 23Dec1863-26Aug1865
Conrad, Jacob J.--47MO Inf,29Aug1864-29Mar1865
Thacker, Louis--40KY MtdInf,20Aug1863-20Dec1864
Leadbetter,No First Name--76ILL Inf,05Aug1862-22Jul1865
Stonton, Frederick A.--24NY Inf,08May1861-22Jul1865
Grantham, Noah--50MO Inf,01Oct1864-23Apr1865
Hembree, Joseph C.--1US VolInf 24Feb1864-10May1866

Woods, John H.--17IND Inf,widow Minervus
Whitehead, Fred. F--35KAN Cav,10Mar1862-05Mar1865
Frymire, Jasper--87ILLMtdInf,14Aug1862-16Jun1865
Murdock, Lindsay--50MO Inf,14Feb1865-05Aug1865
Snyder, Agzo C.--15ILL Cav,01Sep1861-01Sep1864
Poe, James K.—MOMtdCav,28Jan1862-28Feb1865
Wann, John C.--17ILL Inf,01May1861-30Apr1862
Baker, George W.--Fremont'sRangers (MO), 13Aug1864-01Mar1865
Tankersley, Thomas--6MOVolCav,13Aug1864-13Mar1865
Hahn, Jesse--3MOMtdCav,14Feb1864-14Jul1865
Baker, Henry --2MO Cav,10Aug1863-10Dec1865
Hill, Wily W.--8KAN Cav,20Aug1862-09Sep1863
Maloney, William--35Kan Cav
Vance,Robert--5MOMtdCav
Rhodes, Robert--11ILL Inf,15Aug1862-28Jul1865
McGee, Sam T.--6MO Inf,16Jun1861-16Jun1864
Murphy, Patrick--14ILL Cav,22Jan1864-26Jan1865
McKelvy, Elijah--1ARK Inf,20Jun1862-20Jan1863
Rhodes, Samuel--12MO Cav,08Mar1862-05Mar1865
Potter, Leonadis--21ILL Inf,05Nov1861-07Mar1865
Conbire, Robert--31IND Inf,09Sep1861-29Feb1863
Yats, Samuel M.--3MO Cav,Oct1861---Jan1863
Minter, Martin B.--12KY Cav,18Jan1864-23Aug1865
Lincoln, Levi M.--12MO Cav,16Aug1862-16Sep1863
Limbaugh, William M.--6MOVolCav,13Aug1864-13Mar1865
Bortz, Edwin W.--101OHIO Inf,08Aug1862-19Jun1865
Gibbs, Adolphus L.--65ILL Inf,01Jun1862-05Jun1865
Richards, Claborn C.--79MO Cav,13Aug1864-03Mar1865
Shirley, William H.—No Unit Given,1865-served 4 months
Francis, Bird L.—No Unit Given, Jul1861---1865

McGuire, John F.--22IOWA Inf,18Jun1862---1865,widow Sarah R.
Smith, William J.--56ILL Inf,24Jan1864-12Aug1865, widow Mary B.
Caby, Frederick--3MO Cav, widow Margarett
Hahn, Jesse Sen.--MO Inf., served 3 years
Dees, John W.--49ILL Inf,Oct1861---Oct1862,,widow Eliza A.
Sutherland, Pilson M.--9MO Cav, 03Jan1862-16Jul1865
Shell, Phillip--MO Inf,July 1861, widow Catharine
McCardell, Patrick--5MO Cav,Aug1861---Jan1864, former widow Emma M. Mille
Eaker, Michael--79MO Cav,Feb1861---Jul1864, former widow Polly A. Key
Eaker, Peter--MO Cav,1864---Jul1864
Eaker, Wesley,MO Cav,1864-01Jul1864
Eaker, Martin--79MO Cav,Aug1864-03Mar1865
Myers, Peter--MO Inf,1864-1865, widow Sarah
Bess, Peter--3MO Cav, Apr1862-Oct1862
Peter, Anton J.--15MO Inf, 04Jul1861-24Jan1863
Liming, Willis--10ILL Cav, 07Nov1863-22Nov1865
Wariner, Wilson--3MO Cav, Apr1862-Oct1862
Smith, William L.--87ILL Inf, 14Aug1862-16Jun1865
Phelps, David L.--60ILL Inf, 07Jan1862-15Feb1863
Dunn, Charles H.--136ILL Inf,1864-1865 7mo.
Clark, George E.--MASS Inf., 12Sep1862-20Aug1863
Murphy, George W.--43PA Inf, 01Sep1861-20Oct1864, widow Sarah A.
Warsen, Archable--146IND Inf, 05Feb1865-30Aug1865
Myrick, Robert--50MO Inf,16Dec1864-07Aug1865, widow Sarah L.
Watkins, William--MO Cav, 1865-1865 3mo.
Dunkin, Samuel N.--59IND Inf, 05Aug1862-24Dec1863
Lutie, Eli--79MO Cav,Aug1864-03Mar1865
Hicks, John B.--6MO Cav, 1861, former widow Sarah E. Clark
Jaques, Andrew R.--89OHIO Inf, 13Aug1862-06Nov1863
Kinder, _____--MO Cav,1865 6mo., widow Luvenia A.
Turner, Reuben W.--82OHIO Inf, 17Feb1864-24Jul1865
Smith, James J.--18ILL Inf, 21Mar1864-14Dec1865, former widow Sarah J. Crafton
Smith, Anderson--IOWA Inf,1863-1865
Stickler, John—No Unit Given, 3 years

Shelton, Elijah--79MO Cav,Aug1864-03Mar1865;62MO Cav, Nov1863---Jun1864
Crites, Adam--21MO Inf, 20Aug1862-21Aug1865
Shell, Anthony--79MO Cav,Aug1864-03Mar1865
Abernathy, Mathew--21MO Inf,Aug1862---Aug1865
Stem, Christian--70KAN Cav,21Feb1865-29Sep1865
Adams, Wilburn--MO Cav,Jun1862------1865, former widow Cyntha Eaker
Eaker, John E.--,79MO Cav,Aug1864--14days
Eaker, Thomas A. J.--79MO Cav,13Aug1864-03Mar1865
Fowler, Anderson--79MO Cav,13Aug1864-03Mar1865,former widow Lucinda J. Eaker
Eaker, Henry Sr.--79MO Cav,13Aug1864-03Mar1865
Liley, Marston--79MO Cav,13Aug1864-03Mar1865
Virgin, Anderson—No Unit Given, widow Mary
McGregor, Henly P.--15KY Cav,11Aug1862-06Oct1863
Eaker, James H.--49MO Cav,1865-03Mar1865--1 mo.
Lutes, John--49MO Cav,1864--1865 6 mo., former widow Hannah Francis
Delinger, John E.--49MO Cav,Aug1864--03Mar1865
McCairs, William P.--3MO Cav,Aug1861-Mar1864
Masters, Christopher M.--56th MO Inf,Sep1862--Dec1864
__uterrs, Thomas--47MO Inf,25Aug1864--29Mar1865
Har_er, John F.--55OH Inf, 17Oct1864--29Jun1865
Mayer, Alvaris--4MO Cav,1862
James, Levi B.--MO Cav
Winter, Robert--17IL Inf,27Aug1861--01Jun1862
Winter, Robert--66OH Inf,10Aug1864--06Jul1865
Fitzpatrick, Soloman W.--63IL Inf,1862—1865,former widow Jane Sandy
Hatcher, Elery P.--MO Cav,1862—1865, widow Margaret J.
Lane, Cyrus H.--4Indep Co. OH Cav,26Jul1862--28May1865
Boan, John--1IL Cav, 06Jul1861-- Jul1862
Sander, August--4MO Inf, Sep1861--Feb1862;5MO Cav, 22Mar1862--22Mar1865
Glaspel, Louis--31IL Inf,16Jun1861--12Mar1862
Maloney, Phillip--35KY Cav, Nov1862----1864

Kauffman, Isaac--47IL Inf, 16Aug1861--11Oct1864
Bedwell, Andrew J.--30MO Inf,17Jun1862--27Mar1863
Bedwell, Andrew J.--6MO Cav, 01Jan1864-16Mar1865
Huskey, William--9TN Cav,Sep1863----Sep1865
Billings, William--MO Inf

Marble Hill, Lorance Township, Bollinger County MO

Fisher, Robert W.--5MO Cav,12Oct1863--20Mar1865
Menninger, August V.--49MO Cav,Aug1864----Mar1865
Rees, Samuel--MO Cav,1862----1865, former widow Mary Poston
Bery, Henry L.--56MO Cav,Jul1864--11Dec1864
Cole, James W.--60IL Inf,1861--04Jul1864, former widow Nancy W. Johns
Winters, Benjamin F.--49MO Cav,1864--03Mar1865
Janssen, Arland--49MO Cav,1864--03Mar1865
Bair, William H.--146IN Inf,25Jan1865--22Aug1865
Rose, Henry--3MO Inf,7Oct1861--28Oct1864
Williams, Elias—No Unit Given,1862--1865
Saladin, William--18OH Inf,14Feb1862--13Feb1865
Saladin, William--195OH Inf,04Mar1865--18Dec1865
Masters, Daniel M.--MO Inf,1862-1862--1mo.
Masters, George W.--MO Inf,1864-1865--6mo.
Norman, William H.--IL Inf,1862-1865
Mitchell, George--3WI Inf,May1862--Apr1865
Crader, Jackson M.--49MO Cav, Aug1864--Mar1865
Allen, Robert M.--49MO Cav, 1864--1865
Hightower, William J.--20US Inf,13Oct1864--10Nov1865
Clifford, Andrew--56MO Cav,1864-1864 1mo.
Clifford, John F.--Kansas Cav, widow Martha
Armagast, William K.--84PA Inf, Nov1861—1862, former widow Sarah E. Clifford
Penturf, John H.--56MO Cav,1864—1864, widow Sarah C.

Liberty, Bollinger Co. MO

Barrett, Samuel A.--79MO Cav,1Aug1864--1865
Shell, Johnson M.--Fremont Rangers(MO),1Aug61-1Dec61;12MO Cav,Dec1861--21Dec1862
    3MO Cav   12Dec1861--31Dec1865

Rastator, John H.--20MO Inf, 06Jul1861--06Oct1862
Johnson, William--81IL Inf,26Aug1862--25Aug1863, widow Lydia Johnson
Zimmerman, Samuel J.--30MO Inf,22Aug1862--08Aug1865
Collins, Henderson L.--3MO Cav,15Aug1863--15Jul1865
Myers, Joseph W.--3MO Cav,28Dec1863--13Jul1865
Perkins, Peter--13IL Cav,1863--1865
Bidwell, Henry--3MO Cav,12Dec1861--31Jan1865
Rainey, Sears--67IN Inf,18Aug1862--08Aug1863
Wallis, Wiley W.--2MO Lt Arty 07Aug1863--27Aug1865
Shryock, George W.--80IN Inf,10Aug1862--18May1865
Long, Amos T.--60IN Inf,09Jan1862--16Aug1863
James, Randolph --3MO Cav
Sands, Charles E.--107OH Inf,12Aug1862--13Jun1865
Baker, Joseph E.--49IN Inf,21Nov1861--29Nov1864;145IN Inf,21Feb1865--21Feb1866
Virgin, Enoch--MO Cav
Hindman, Monroe--11IN Inf,28Sep1863--19Sep1865
Shell, Troy W.--3MO Cav,03Jan1862--31Jan1865, widow Nancy C.
Pickett, Hiram A.--12MO Cav,Jan1862--Jul1862
Williams, William W.--2MO Inf,28Jul1861--10Oct1864
Shell, Alfred--3MO Cav,22Jul1863--13Jul1865
Hahn, Jacob W. G.—No Unit Given, widow Margaret C.
Fee, John--56OH Inf,26Sep1861--24Mar1866
Nevins,William--FremontRangers(MO),10Jul61-10Dec1861;12MOCav,12Dec1861-30Jan1865
Gevins, William H.--2IL Lt.Arty 02Mar1862--02Mar1865
Crismore, George W.--87IN Inf,09Aug1862--12Jul1865
Wallace, John--50IN Inf,19Jan1864--13Feb1865
Fowler, Henry M.--3MO Cav,22Jul1863--13Jul1865
Brooks, Coryden--US Soldier
Strill, Charles--49OH Inf,16Aug1861-5Sep1862
Strill, Charles--65OH Inf,26Sep1864--16Jan1865
McCarver, William--31IL Inf,Nov1861--3 months, former widow Massina Mallory
Curdley, James H.--22IN Inf,01Sep1864--04Feb1865

Bass, Jefferson--At home with family could not go in service
Moore, Albert--2MO Lt.Arty,1864-1865
Johnson, John--1st Engineers(MO),1861-1864
Neminger, Charles--2IL Lt Arty,1861-1867
Coleman, Isac F.--33MO Inf,1862-1865
Allero, Christen--8MO Inf,1861-1864
Brown, William H. H.--167OH Inf,1864-1864
Elon, Francis--29IL Inf,1862-1865
Green, Lebell--8IN Inf,1862-1865
Miller, John A.--13PA Cav,1861-1864
Worts, William G.--25IN Inf,1861-1865
Ahum, Patrick--90IL Inf,1862-1865
Corey, Barney J.----No Unit Given,Soldier
Crites, Conrad—No Unit Given,Soldier

Fillmore Township Bollinger County MO

Cooper, John M.--3MO Cav,22Jul1863--13Jul1865
Cooper, Thomas H.--MO Cav,01Jul1864--1865
Reece Nehemiah E.--MO Cav,01Jul1864--1865
Cooper, Thomas J.--79MO Cav,29Oct1862--1865
Collins, Trion W.--10TN Inf,Apr1863--03Jul1865
Robins, Samuel--12MO Cav,12Nov1861-04Feb1863
Tally, Green B.--14IL Cav, Feb1864-17Jul1865
Reece, Joseph E.--79MO Cav,29Oct1862--June1863
Rece, Joseph E.--47MO Inf,17Aug1864--28Mar1865
Stovall, William P.--47MO Inf,17Aug1864--28Mar1865
Monroe, Allison H.--3MO Cav,17Feb1864--25Oct1864;14MO Cav,25Oct1864--26Oct1865
Gray, James G.--48IL Inf,Sep1861--Jan1864
Allen, John C.--97IN Inf,19Jul1862--09Jun1865
Pound, Thomas F.--128IN Inf,02Jan1864--24Mar1865
Guinn, Levi C.--KY Cav
Abernathy, David A.--3MO Cav,22Jul1863--13Jul1865, former widow Marie Damille
Robins, John D. L.--3MO Cav,12Dec1861--31Jan1868
James, John--3MO Cav,1861--12Sep1863, widow Sally E.
Patterson, William--27IN Inf,12Aug1861--Feb1863
Patterson, William--136IN Inf,May1864--Sep1864
Sh_licker, Christopher C.--MO Cav,May1864-Sep1864
Jackson, John--8MO Cav,1861-1864
Phillips, Charley--TN Inf,1864--Jul1865

Comelison, Andrew F.--56IL Inf,Oct1862--June1863, former widow Sarah C. Sitze
Lurribeth, Benjamin F.--48PA Inf, 23Apr1861--Apr1865
Finley, Solomon D.--50MO Inf,01Aug1864--21Mar1865
Whitener, Henry B.--MO Cav,Mar1862--1862
Hedrich, Casper--MO Cav,Mar1864--1864 6mo., widow Ann
Rush, Fenjamin F.--2MO Inf,10Sep1861--27Sep1864
Pennick, Samuel--16OH Inf,02May1864--02Sep1864
Nichols, Elias--IN Inf, 29Sep1864--21Mar1865, former widow Nancy J. Pennick

Wayne Township Bollinger County Missouri

Cato, Nathan L.--79MO Inf,07Jul1864--28Feb1865
Cubbage, Julius C.--23OH Inf, 08Feb1864--Jul1865
Walker, Haiden--147IL Inf,30Jan1865-1865 11mo., widow Mariah Walker
Fears, William --79MO Inf,07Jul1864--38Feb1865
Warnack, Frances M.--6MO Cav,01Sep1861--06Sep1864
Sullivan, James L.--15OH Inf,16Nov1862-17Jul1865, former widow Pursiah Warnack
Gaines, Henry--30MO Cav,02Dec1861--31Jan1865
_____ < James W.--Fremont Rangers(MO),Sep1861--Dec1861
Bess, Peter--12MO Cav,Mar1862--Feb1863
Kinder, Emanuel--79MO Cav, 04Jul1864--Feb1865
Davis, Alford--175OH Inf,05Sep1864--27Jun1865
Cato, Ransom--79MO Cav,07Jul1864--28Feb1865
Cot, Mahalan--4Col,11Aug1862--29Jun1865
Lincoln, Andrew G.--14MO Cav,11Apr1865--17Nov1865
Grant, Joseph H.--110OH Inf,24Aug1862--13Jun1865
Burkhead, Elleazer--6TN Cav, 20Jul1863--15May1865

Garision, Obdiah--50MO Inf,03Oct1864--07Aug1865,former widow Sarah E. Tully
Hall, David--12MO Cav,07Jul1862--Mar1863
Shrader, Josep--6MO Cav,Aug1861--Oct1864, widow Sarah C.
Taylor, John--97IN Inf,20Jul1862--09Jun1865
Luny, Joseph L.--2TN Inf,11Nov1861--26Nov1864
Wait, James W.--21IL Inf, Jun1861--Aug1864
Hinkle, Michael--47KY Inf,Aug1864--Mar1865, widow Elizabeth
Smith, Francis M.—No Unit Given
Charles, Andrew J.--92IN Inf,Sep1865--Aug1865
Gobble, Anderson--2TN Cav,08Nov1862--06Jul1865
Mackin, Cox--47IN Inf,21Nov1861--24Oct1864, widow Margretta C.
Jackson, James H--2IL Arty,10Jan1863--Apr1865
Heuton, A. J.--6TN Inf,May1864--July1865
Lacy, John G.--47MO Inf,17Aug1864--28Mar1865
Hale, Jeremiah--8MO Cav,24Oct1862--27Aug1865
Fish, James M.--47MO Inf,06Aug1864--28Mar1865
Fish, Thomas M.--47MO Inf,18Aug1864--28Mar1865
Davis, Crouch--143IL Inf,27May1864--28Sep1864
Wells, Elias--2MO Arty,14Mar1864--28Dec1865
Starz, Luis--5MO Cav,Sep1861--Feb1868
Martin, George W.--7US,Jul1874--04Aug1879
Virgin, Edzriah--2MO,May1863--Aug1865
Wilkins, Lindsey--59IN,Jan1862--Apr1868, former widow Virginia Thanauson
Borders, David G.--47MO Inf,Aug1864--Mar1865
Deck, John—No Unit Given
Sylcox, George W.--3MO Cav,Jul1863--Oct1865
Chuk, John--3MO Cav,15Dec1863--Nov1865, widow Margrett J.

BUTLER COUNTY MISSOURI

Census records here use standard abbreviations for states known at the time. Inf stands for infantry, Cav stands for cavalry, Mtd stands for Mounted, Art stands for artillery," " indicates a ship name, (Confed) indicates confederate which had a line drawn through the entry as this was a Union Veterans census. There are soldiers listed in a few other southern states which also could be Confederate but did not have the lines drawn through the entry. There also appears to be some duplication of names—some with and without units. Also some units from southern states were Union Units.

NAME—Unit/Ship
Harvey, Thomas--47 MO Inf
Pearce, Rebeca former widow of Wm. H. Niagauer--3 Ind. Cav
Slater, Mary C. widow of Silas Slater--12 Ind. Inf
Luse, Julia, formerly widow of James A. Raspberry--   No unit given
Luse, John H. alias John M. Garry--1st Class Boy "Ouchita"
Judy, widow of Elivis ___higua--4 Col Inf
Elizabeth Walker formerly widow of Allen Watts--MO Cav
House, Thomas-- 6 ND Cav
Neal, Alfred J.--10 TN Cav
Brown, John alias Elwood Smith--No unit given
Cook, Willis--US nd
Williams, Mary formerly widow of George Bluff--4 Col Inf
Darker, Joel O.-- Franklin Co. Regt Home Guard R.C. MO
George, Thomas J.--24 MO Inf, 21 MO Inf
Fludder, John A.--129 Ind. Inf
Hiuricks, Charles F. Sr.--10 MO Cav
Reeves, Melinda formerly widow of Benjamin Edwards--No unit given
Renfro, Dora formerly widow of Ferdinand Yeager--7 Ill Inf
Eckstein, John Eat.--US Cav
Granger, Ann E. formerly widow of Ambers Ship--11 KY Inf
Ewing, Charles E.--6 KS Cav
Morgan, E. M. formerly widow of William H. Morgan--No unit given
Palmer, Joseph--ll MO Inf
Garetson, James L.--62 Ill Inf
Richards, Stephen S.--No Unit given
Zender, John G. alias Zender, George--123 PA Inf
Smith, Samuel W.--No Info given
Riley, John--No unit given
Kellogg, James M.--8 Ind Cav, 39 Ind Inf
Kellogg, James--54 Ind Inf

Frederick, Louis--18 MO Inf, Drummer 2 MO Inf
Shepherd, Charles--151 NY Inf
Perkins, Leroy A.--No Info given
West, David F.--4 PA Inf, 4 US Inf
Williams, James M.--6 US Inf
Bishop, Charles G.--16 Ohio Inf
Grinder, Charles H.--No Info given
Niles, Ambrose B.--31 Ill Inf, Hosp Stew 77 Ill Inf
Smith, William M. alias William Beattner--60 US Col Inf
Houston, Louisa formerly widow of Prince Fairlane--   No info given
Walters, Joseph W.--19 PA Cav
Smithers, Andrew F.--49 Ill Inf
Gnan (Gnau), George K.--195 PA Inf
Conrad, James A.--62 Ohio Inf
Buxton, Richard A.--No Info given
Nickey, Leander F.--93 Ind. Inf, 15 Mich
Davidson, Isaac M.--1LT--31 MO Inf
Sirrious, Henry G.--2 MO Lt. Art.
Frelinau, Mortimer L.--No Info given
Shendaw, William--Landsman "Wauchusetts"
Leuer, Henry C.--150 Ohio Home Guard
Robinson, Andrew C.--US Soldier
Fenneny, Richard--US Soldier
Moore, John W. --US Soldier
Locks, Eli C.--US Soldier
Mills, Lemuel--US Soldier
Gorch, John A.--81 Ill Inf
Buckley, Calvin N.--7 KS Cav
Dowd, Lemuel--144 Ill
Stark, Jemima former widow of Albert Nuchell--Ind.
Robinson, Martha A. widow of Richard Robinson--Ohio
Margaret widow of Duncan--16 Ill Cav
Peterson, John L. --Capt--149 Ill Inf
King, Charles A.--48 Ill Inf
Green, John B--No Info given
Slater, Benjamin B.--80 Ill Inf
Slater, Mary, former widow of Charles Bilderback--40 Ill Inf

Baskey, Peter--10 Ohio Cav
Reed, James B.--No Info given
Davidson, Joseph, F.--No Info given
Holt, Eliza J. widow of Anderson Holt--124 Ohio Inf
Elizabeth, widow of Franz--No Info given
Shackle, William--62 Ill Inf
Baker, Hood S.--No Info given
Randles, James T.--143 Ohio Inf
Harmon, Michael L--30 Ill Inf
Brown, John H.--11 MO Inf
Goodlander, Henry--36 Ind. Inf
Martin, Taylor--17 KY
Harlan, Horace F.--10 ME
Willson, William H.--6 Ill Cav
Romine, Robt.--14 Ohio Inf
Romine, R. F.--182 (132) Ohio Inf
Bunlow, David C.--2 KS Cav
Martha A. Buxton formerly widow of Venlus, John-- No Info given
Livingston, Edward U.—2LT--56 Ind. Inf
Silkwood, William M.--59 Ill Inf
Burkett, William M.--11 Ill Inf
Newton, Frances M.--No Info given
Hill, Absolum B. --188 Ohio Inf
Payton, John--No Info given
Foust, John--72 Ind. Inf
Ackerman, Louis--37 Ohio Inf
Ashcraft, Willis-- 48 KY Inf
Nancy J. Stringer formerly widow of Thorn Halloran--48 Ill Inf
Howard, Samuel L.--97 Ill Inf
Nancy E. Markham formerly widow of James L. Scott--30 MO Inf
Stone, Thomas J.--18 Ohio Inf
May (Way), William J.--130 Ind. Inf
Barryanluer, John P.--14 Ill Cav
Burcille, S. Bachtell formerly widow of Barryanleur, Andrew J.--5 Ill Cav
Rose, James M.-- Capt.--48 Ind. Inf
Mary L. widow of Sacklis, J. B.--No Info given
Davidson, William B--54 Ill Inf
Isabelle widow of Benjamin Wynn--10 Ill Cav
Timmons, Ira B.--17 KY
Clanton, John--29 Ill Inf
Beraray, Henry W.--2 Mich Inf
Smith, Alfred--11 MO Inf
Myres, George F--24 Ind. Inf
Hull, Franklin P.--PA Inf
Kesler, Frank--183 Ohio Inf
Kittredge, Dewitt C.--No Info given
Dalton, Amaziah --8 Ind. Inf
Reed, John W.--27 Ill Inf
Martha Landers formerly widow of William Parain--No Info given
Tensi, John __.-- 2 Kansas

Mary Hill former widow of John L. Tanner--78 PA Inf
Janaway, Newton N.--MO
_____, Samuel --KS
Smith, James--16 KY Cav
Geiza J. widow of Chambers--31 KY Inf
Keltrain, James A.--6 MO Cav
Barnes, John--33 MO Inf
Beasley, William H.--71 Ohio Inf
Carter, Benjamin--59 Ill Inf
Shadle, George W.--62 Ill Inf
Felkins, Thomas S.--11 Ill Inf
Hedinger, William B--192 PA Inf
Morris, Levi--48 Ill Inf
Elliot, Robert R.--No Info given
Larkin, Mathew-- No Info given
Irby, James W.--6 Ill Inf
Rebecca J. widow of Gideon J. Phealinge--18 Ill Inf
Alice widow of Charles Witt--No Info given
Susan M. widow of Isaac F. Hatfield--144 Ind Inf
Scott, James P.--3 TN Mtd. Rifles
Holt, Dowrey--12 MO Inf
Hill, George W.--6 MO Inf
Goreby, John B.—Bugler--3 MO Cav
Suttons, John--17 Ind. Inf
Duff, John W.--No Info given
Harress, Edward J.--2 MO Inf
McElroy, Phelix-- NY Cav
Martin, John M.--5 VA
Mary widow of Thomas March--LA Inf
Ford, Lewis M.--1st Miss Inf
Catharine widow of Adam Surben--149 Ind. Inf
Hannah formerly widow of Noah Prickett--10 Ill Cav
Watkins, John--73 Ill Inf
McDaniel, James--No Info given
Catharine widow of Franklin--No Info given
Griffith, Jasper--136 Ind. Inf
Griffith, Thomas J.--58 Ind. Inf
Davison, Joseph F.-- Ill Cav
Roland, Oliver T.--No Info given
House, R. C.--29 Ill Inf, 62 Ill Inf
Long, Samuel--56 Ill Inf
Dowdy, Mary E--Soldier's widow
Levtz, E.R.--Yes
Kent, George H.--US Soldier
Gooch, H. A.--US Soldier
Burreth, Isaac--US Soldier
Elizabeth Annully formerly widow of John M. Moar--12 MO Cav
Elizabeth Nunley widow of Nunley--No Info given
Clear, James--19 Ohio Inf

Sarah Caldwell former widow of _____, William H.--No Info given
Caldwell, Joshua--10 TN Inf
Barrett, Ambrose --Seaman--"Mound City"
Porch, Joseph--31 MO Inf
Casey, George W.--32/31 MO Inf
Davenport, Lewis F--No Info given
Burket, Robert--47 MO Inf
Clayton, William H--3 Ohio Inf, 24 Ohio Inf, 18 Ohio Inf
Hester, Melissa former widow of Jacob White--26 MO Inf
Thing, Charles W.--1 ME Inf, 14 ME Inf, 83 USG Inf
Burress, George W.--51 Ind. Inf
Mercer, David--1 West VA Light Art.
Harrison, William H.--20 Ohio Inf
Matilda J. Ramsey former widow of Thomas Tapp--No Info given
Autry, Benjamin F.--17 KY Inf
Sarah Cooper former widow of Caswell R. Cooper--No Info given
Innman, Shadrick--3 MO Cav
Jane H. Innman former widow of Jacob W. Meadows--No Info given
Morgan, William H.--8 Ind. Inf
Childers, Major L.--31 MO Inf
Carpenter, John W.--11 Ark Cav
Mary A. Carpenter former widow of William C. Tackett--3 MO Cav
Holt, George M-- 6 MO Inf
Mary J. Holt, former widow of William M. Powell--5 Ill Cav
Looksbill, Peter O.--70 Ind. Inf
Davidson, Hugh C. --Capt.--No Info given
Rebecca J. Reese former widow of Charles W. Reess--47 MO Inf
Elizabeth Barnes former widow of James W. Allman--31 MO Inf
Martha J. Mathis former widow of Ephraim C. Rowlis___--MO
Woodruff, Benjamin--31 MO Inf
Edminston, John--Ohio
Frees, Charles--7 KS Cav, 12 MO Cav
Saluda E. Whitworth former widow of Elvie T. Whitworth--No Info given
Mary Hartman former widow of _____ Hartman--111 Ill Inf
Talid, William--2 TN Inf
Louisa Collins former widow of William P Collins--9 TN Cav
Wagaman, James J.--49 MO Inf
Emily Baker former widow of Stephen Bachis—Blacksmith--6 MO Cav
Sarah R. Hamilton--No Info given
Adams, John E.--8 Ill Inf

Feverstone, Edwin--51 Ill Inf
Lane, Susan widow –Surgeon--3 Ill Cav
Harrison, John M.--LT.--81 Ind. Inf
Janes, Samuel J.--85 Ind. Inf
Miller, William--10 Ill Inf
Huckaby, Persom M.--MO Art.
Wood, Jonathan--24 MO Inf
Wiley, Josiah--50 MO Inf
Alberty, Nathan--2 MO Cav
Kittrell, Lemerick C.--50 MO Inf
Williams, Byard--12 Ohio Inf, 5 Ohio Cav
Hodge, Aaron F.--5 Kansas Cav
Shaffer, Leonard --1 Kan. Inf
Huitt, John M.--No Info given
McGaven, Benjamin F.--No Info given
Lookingbill, Samuel E.--No Info given
Naills, George E. --26 Mich Inf
Luce, John S--Ind.
Riece, Mathew G.--10 Ind. Inf
Smith, Reuben D.--Co. B--No other info
Lewis, William A.--150 Ill Inf
Rupper, Christopher--115 Ill Inf
Burton, John T.--140 Ind. Inf
Purdy, Elden--10 Wis. Inf
Roberts, John W.-- Co F-- 3 (Ind. Cav, MO Cav, Ohio Inf)
Smith, Robert L.--6 KY Cav
Dowdy, Thomas W--10 Ind. Cav
Perkins, Simson--54 Ill Inf
Gibson, Duane B.--12 KY Inf
Thorn, James R.--MO Vol
Sarah E. Gourley widow of John D. Gourley--48 MO Inf
Elizabeth Foster widow of James Ubank--110 Ill Inf
Burke, Dan L.--47 MO Inf
Scaggs, John W--(Confederate)
Henderson, William J.--(Confederate 4 TN Inf)
Vaughn, Robert--(Confederate 7 KY Cav)
Moore, Jacob M.--(Confederate 7 Ark)
Ingram, John W. --1LT--25 Ind. Inf
Owen, Thomas R.--8 Ark Inf
Mazear Pratt former widow of David Blogg--5 Ill
Huston, Joseph L.--144 Ill Inf
Lucy Owen widow of KY Owen--(Confederate)
Smith, Elijah O.--27 Ind. Inf
Shuler, David--(Confederate 37 Virginia Inf)
Sarah C. Lannsberg widow of Lansberg--No Info given
Hudson, B. W.--(Confederate 37 TN Inf)
Floyd, Robert--(Confederate 7 SC Inf)
Tomlin, William R.--(Confederate 3 MO Inf)
Muhuldia Roberts widow of William Roberts--No Info given
Harrott, Robert--(Confederate SC)
Foister, Mike O.--No Info given

Delida Hanie widow--No Info given
Arthur, James--No Info given
Mary Helterbrand widow of Isaac--(Confederate)
Evelease Pierce widow of Pierce--(Confederate)
Missouri Mayse widow--(Confederate)
Blow, Daniel--(Confederate)
Glass, Marion--No Info given
Malinda Young widow of--No Info given
Alfred, Kelley—LT--14 MO Inf, 2 MO Inf
Barneheart, Schluter--85 MO Mtd Inf
Anny Filkin widow of Henry Filkin--25 Ind. Inf
Franklin Roggers--80 Ind. Inf
John Wilson --6 MO Cav
John W. Jackson--1 Ill Art
John Snuffin--63 Ill Inf
John L. Wand--37 Ill Inf
William D. Lewis--US soldier
Peter Peterson--US soldier
Jesse B. Brown--US soldier
John R. Hayes--US soldier
George Eaker--US soldier
Jonathan Scott--US soldier
Isam Crilly--US soldier
Margaret Wright widow--US soldier
Joseph H. Winder--No Info given
John W. Cooker--No Info given
John Hicks--No Info given
John W. Cooker--No Info given
Mary J. Henson widow--No Info given
Elijah R. Cookmont--No Info given
William R. Hunter--No Info given
Hamlin Jones--No Info given
Mary Jane Baggott widow--No Info given
Stephen Bagwell--No Info given
James A. Jackson--No Info given
Thomas J. Davidson--2nd Regt (No state given).
Woolman, Lorranza D.--1 Ill Art
Hiacock, Malon--58 Ind. Inf
Avery, William H.--49 Ill Inf
Alsman, Andrew--149 Ind. Inf
Good, Jeremiah--33 Ind. Inf
Chaffin, Aaron--12 KY Cav
Hamlin Jones--43 Ind. Inf
Nancy Wright formerly widow of Groundville, James S.--MO Inf
Jackson, James H.--31 MO Inf
Bagwell, Stephen --12 TN Cav
Crinsthu Aramor formerly widow of W. C. Houston--17 Ill Cav
Charlotte Heath widow of Marchall H. Heath--20 Col. Cav
Hayes, John A.--12 MO Cav
Winder, Joseph W.--87 Ill Inf
Mary Ann Davis former widow of A. J. Swafford--Ill Inf
Mabory, M.--87 Ill Inf

Amandy Mehorigsby, former widow of James Pate-- MO Inf
Pasaneter, W. A. --24 Ind Inf
Eliza Cook widow of J. H. Cook--17 KY Cav
Hunter, W. R.--73 MO Cav
Hicks, James--150 Ill Inf
Brown, J. B.--6 MO Cav
Eaker, G.--15 Mo Inf
Hicks, J.--49 Ill Inf
Maryann Wright former widow of J. Driskill--33 Ill Art
Crilly, J.--58 Ind. Inf
Scott, J. --78 Ind. Inf
Cooper, W--79 Ind. Inf
Yarbrough, G.--17 KY Inf
Nancy Jane Baggott widow--No Info given
Della Jordan widow--No Info given
Mary J. Henson widow--No Info given
Hogue (Hogan), Samuel A.--40 Ill Inf, 13 Ill Cav
Parthena E. Epps former widow of David W. Hill--6 MO Inf
Mary L. widow of Willis D. Gully--50 Ill Inf
John Smith--27 Iowa Cav
Daniel Harlow--93 Ill Inf
Mary A. Stout former widow of Benjamin F. Gregory--No Info given
Henry White--4 KY Mtd. Inf
George H. Cox--80 Ind. Inf
William Smith--30 Ind. Inf
Jennie Ivy widow of Henry Ivy--20 KY Inf
Elizabeth T. McCullah former widow of John Harris--3 Ind. Inf
Matilda McCrary former widow of Zachariah Selby--6 Ind Inf
James Hamilton--10 MO Cav
George N. Persons--17 Ken Cav
Mary H. Brake former widow of Samuel H. Priest--32 MO Inf
Andrew J. Dunning--65 Ind. Inf
Ezekiel A. Counts--197 Ohio Inf
Daniel Smith--7 TN Cav
Elizabeth Wisdom former widow of Anderson Ward--47 MO Inf
Nicholas Meyers--MO Cav
Henry G. Wilson--1 Ill Art
Willis Roe--50 MO Inf
Nathaniel B. Williams--120 Ill Inf
Louisa J. Lewis former widow of William L. Phillips--48 Ill Inf
Melissa Franklin former widow of William Rigor--6 MO Cav
John Gavin-87 Ill Mtd Inf
Hardy C. Dicken--120 Ill Inf
Andrew Skinner--7 Ohio Cav
John Maddox--3 Iowa Inf

Berthena Helmerick former widow of Simon P. Borders--81 Ill Inf
Archibald F. Somers--1 TN Mtd. Inf
Henry H. Sickels--22 Ind. Inf
William H. Brown--48 Ill Inf
James L. Jackson --50 Ill Inf
Marion Perry--27 Ind. Inf, 4 US Light Art
William H. Lockewood--20 Ill Inf
James M. Ferguson--13 Ill Cav
Amanda L. Turner widow of Turner--24 Ind. Inf
Lafayette D. Warbington--1 Ala Cav
Charles Bush--No Info given
George Winder--No Info given
Alexander J, McGinnell (McConnell)--No Info given
Thomas H. Hassler--No Info given

The following names were found mixed in with Bollinger County MO:
Fairlow, William C.--29 IL Inf
Everett, Robert S.--43 Ohio Inf
Strout, James W. --MO Cav
Crews, George W.--8 IL Inf
Helm, Marion M. --120 IL Inf
Haney, James H.--17 IN Inf, 60 IN Inf
Evins, William M.--8 IL Inf
Leader, Charles H.--184 Penn Inf

CAPE GIRARDEAU CO. MISSOURI

The following abbreviations were used: MO for Missouri, PA for Pennsylvania, NY for New York, Wisc for Wisconsin, Kan for Kansas, IL for Illinois, Ind for Indiana and IN for Indiana, MSM for Missouri State Militia, Col' and col for colored; Lt for light, Art for artillery, cav for cavalry, inf for infantry, WI for Wisconsin, KY and Ken for Kentucky, OH for Ohio, Mtd for mounted, Mass for Massachusetts, Eng for Engineer, Ark for Arkansas, Vol for volunteer, Mich for Michigan, AR for Arkansas, USS for US soldier, Neb for Nebraska.

The quality of this microfilm was very poor. I have tried to transcribe it to the best of my ability. A large percentage of names were German (fortunately my German helped there). However, if the reader feels there are some inaccuracies, I apologize. The reader may wish to purchase a transcription done by the Cape Girardeau Co. Missouri Historical Society. Since I have not seen their transcription, I can only recommend that you check it out as well as purchasing a copy of the film.

In some cases, names were duplicated or triplcated, I have consolidated these if there was more than one unit listed for the same person. Sometimes first names were first and sometimes last names were first. These names are recorded in like manner here, so be sure to use the edit –find in page of your browser.

Occasionally, the census taker would write down the name before finding out the individual or widow's husband was a Confederate. The census taker would draw a line through the entry, and place a C in the left hand column. I have indicated if the individual or widow's husband was a Confederate.

NAME--UNIT

Sauerbanes, Valentine, MO Home Guards
Haman, Christian , MO Home Guards
Thilenius, George C., MO Home Guards, 56 MO Militia
Slinech, Christian, No Unit Given
Schweitzer, Charles, 26 MO
Arhl, Casper, 56 MO
Fritz, Daniel, 2 IL Lt. Art.
Klaproth, Henry W., 1 MO Eng.
Ford, Joshua L., 54 IL
Smith, William, 2 MO, 13 MO
Keunke, George C., 1 MO Cav
Roth, George H., MO Home Guards
Person, Ellis, 87 IL
Nabe, Henry, 29 MO
Schrock, Charles, 79 MO
Grawden, John , 1 MO Lt. Art
Abernathie, William, US Sol, no unit given
Pierson, Mary, Widow of US soldier, no unit given
Grawden, Lizzie, Widow of US soldier, no unit given
Farrar, Mahalia, Widow of US soldier, no unit given
Kaiser, Henry W., No Unit Given
Elbrecht, John C., No Unit Given
Rissennis, George P., 56 MO
Zoelluer, No First Name Given, 56 MO
Dawback, Jacob, 56 MO
Richter, Henry F., 56 MO
Raiffer, Rupple, 56 MO
Crites, William D., 56 MO
Bohnist, Charles, 56 MO
Meidenhoff, Auton, 56 MO
Wills, Peter, 56 MO
Bailey, John, 56 MO
Zimmermann, Wm., 3 MO Cav.
_asolius widow of William Guisek, No Unit Given
Oebel, Frederick, Engineer Regt. Of West
The___ Oebel former widow of Casper Vogt, Unit Not given
Grosheider, John F, No Unit Given
Moeller, Christian F., 3 MO Inf, 1 East MO Militia
Puntissann, William, 5 MO
Zocke, Adolph, No Unit Given
Bingeralennan, George, No Unit Given
Schulz, Frederick, 32 WI Inf
Wilke, Frederick, 4 MO Inf
Middleton, David, 56 MO, 7 MO, 2 MO
Hiltenbrand, George W., 4 MO, 8 MO, 2 MO Lt. Arty
Gebleard, Lewis, 1 MO Home guard
Buckingham, Auton, 8 _____
Christine Crumholz widow of Bernard Crumholz, 4 MO Inf
Ruch, Aaron, No Unit Given
Burkbulgler, Jacob, Pvt. Co. H No Unit given
Diamond, Wm., Pvt. No Unit Given
Bricker, Christian, MO State Militia

Bernhard, Ki__, No Unit Given
Mary Glaub widow of John Glaub, No Unit Given
Mary Wel_mueller, No Unit Given
Henry Hartwig, 5 MO State Militia
Wagner, Philip, 6 US Inf, 4 MO Inf
Hildebrand, Emanuel, 47 MO Inf
Kabeck, William, 15 IL Cav
Hales, Henry W., 5 MO Cav
Haupt, Christian C., 1 MO Inf
Theesse Oudl widow of Casper Vogt, No Unit Given, repeat from earlier listing
Stoffreque, Henry, Soldier
Mueller, Christoph, 56 MO Cav
Mary E. Meyer widow of Frederick Meyer, 56 MO Cav
Oxen, Frederick, 56 MO Cav
Fuschhoff, Henry, 56 MO Cav
Schremok, George, 56 MO Cav
Minerva Shoults widow of John A. Shouts, 12 MO State Militia
Damback, Frederick, 8 MO Inf
Cotner, Joseph L., 8 MO Cav
Born, John H., 8 MO Inf
Minerva C. Sider widow of Rufus Sider, 56 MO Cav
Cotner, Wm. W., 56 MO Cav
Rasten, Henry C., 56 MO Cav
Hinkle, Marvin, 56 MO Cav
Hope, Oliver H., 8 MO Cav. (Confederate)
Gerth, Herman, 58 MO Inf.
Schoen, Gustav A., 56 MO
Herman Fe_____, No Unit Given
Weisbrat, Mathias, 8 MO Inf
Thompson, William L., 56 MO Cav
Bowers, John A., 2 MO Lt. Arty
Mary C. Lance widow of James M. Lance, No Unit Given (Confederate)
Reid, John B., 56 MO Cav
Bruick, Henry, 56 MO Cav
Wilson, James E., Pvt. (Confederate)
Cora C. Harris widow of Oliver S. Harris, 8 MO Cav (Confederate)
Martha A. E. Smith widow of Edwin J. Smith, 56 MO Cav
Bowman, Samuel S., 8 MO Inf (Confederate)
Johnson, Cornelius, No Unit Given
Walker, J. H., 8 MO Cav (Confederate)
Kirby, Josep F, No Unit Given
Brown, William L., 5 MO Cav
Hermine Schzlek late widow of Joseph Hain, 2 MO Lt. Arty
Ludwig, Casper, 56 MO Cav
Ect___, John, 56 MO Cav
Schriner, Phillip, 56 MO Cav
Schneider, Frederick, 56 MO Cav

Louisa Lewis widow of Henry Lewis, 56 MO Cav
Arma A. Miller widow of William A. Miller, 56 MO Cav
Kellis Baker, 102 Mich. Inf
Goche, Theodore, 56 MO Cav
Wilkening, William, 56 MO Cav
Kasten, Christian, 56 MO Cav
Willis, Gro___ S., 56 MO Cav
Drum, Louis C., No Unit Given
Mary E. Lang widow of William E. Long (Lang), 56 MO Cav, 50 MO Inf
Summers, Stephen, 2 MO Regt (Confederate)
Seibert, Charles, No Unit Given
Smith, John J., 3 KY Cav
Statler, Henry M., Price's Army (Confederate)
Mary M. Widow of Quilla N. Phelps, 120 IL Inf
Slaughter, William, 3 MO Cav
Thomas, John P., 29 MO Inf
Gloth, Christian, 2 MO Lt Arty
Eakins, Joseph K, 56 MO Cav
Bruhus, William, 12 MO Cav
Lange, Ferdinan, 5 MO Cav
Wilhelmina widow of Henry Honnshildt, 5 Mo Cav
Thomas, Louis F., 2 MO Lt. Arty
Brown, William G., US Soldier, no unit given
Schaefer, Henry, 56 MO
Schaefer, Christian, 56 MO Cav
Sachse, Thomas, 5 MO Cav
Tuschhoff, Bernhard, 56 MO Cav
Schmidt, Frederick W., 1 MO Eng.
Brown, William H., 12 MO Cav
Kaiser, Frederick , 4 MO Inf
Wolfokehles, William, 5 MO Cav
Kohler, Henry, 2 IL Art
Fulbright, John, 12 MO Cav
Etheridge, William, 3 Iowa Cav
Burns, Richard, 5 MO Cav
Campbell, Franklin, No Unit Given
Davis, James F., 2 MO Lt. Arty
Davis, Robert __, 2 MO Cav
Delph, Jacob, 2 MO Lt. Arty
Eggers, Herman, 101 IN Inf
Ford, Robt., 2 MO Lt. Arty
Huder, William, 36 MO Inf
Harding, Joseph E., 30 IL Inf
Kaufmann, George, No Unit Given
Kohler, Christian , 2 IL Lt. Art
Morrison, Robert , 8 MO Cav
Moiri, William H., No Unit Given
Magler, Henry, No Unit Given
Reed, Isaac W., 5 MO Cav
Reynolds, Gabraud, 4 KY Cav
Siemars, John W., 12 __ Cav
John Runl____ , 1 MO Inf

Wenans, Edward, 3 OH Inf Chaplain
Guffey, William, No Unit Given
_____, William G., 35 ___ Inf
_____, E. Sepel, 6 Col. Inf
Susan Wells widow of Alfred Walls, No Unit Given
Schwearb, Henry, 29 IN Inf
Patpr__son, Wentamin, 5 IL Cav
Charles Bleckwendt, 1 MO Inf
Christine K. widow of Peter Bienleiu, 64 MO Inf
Baugh, Joel F., 149 IL Inf
Bauer, Henry, 2nd Independent Mtd. Inf
Bart, Benjamin, 2nd Independent Mtd. Inf
Anderson, Cooley, 46 Mass. Inf
Erinertz, Hugh__ , Cape Girardeau Home Guard Inf
Therese M. widow of William Flenge, 5 MO Cav
Wilhelmina Volkert former widow of Hermani Fredericks, 2 IL Cav
Ford, Ralph P., 3 MO Cav
Grasit, Albert H, 1 Mass Heavy Art
Hoffmeister, Christian, 2 MO Inf
Elizabeth widow of Henry Huron, 56 MO Inf
Harrison, Nashere C., MO Home Guard
Hosly, Ephraim, 3 MO Cav
Henderson, Robert T., 64 MO Inf
Jones, Henry L., 98 IL Inf
Kneipert, Jacob H., 10 KY Inf, &Mississippi Musicians Brigade(Possible Confederate)
Masters, Leander S., 201 PA Inf
May, Frank, 56 MO Inf.
Oldenhoeuer, William, 1 MO Inf
Obermeller, August, 82 IL Inf
Pepper, August, 64 MO Inf
Ruff, Benjamin, MO Inf.
Sauder, Adessa, MO Inf
Steinhoff, Ernst, 1 MO Inf
Schaeter, Jacob H., 1 Nebraska Inf
Umbeck, Ernest, 34 MO Inf
Volkert, Frantz, Cape Girardeau Home Guards
Harriet widow of King Williams, 65 US C Inf
Hamilton, David J., No Unit given
Peck, John, 56 MO
Henrietta widow of Christian Schauthe, 2 ILL Art
Heilner, Henry, Musician US Reserve Corps.
Smock, Nathaniel, No Unit Given
Grube, Sebastian, 1 MO Eng
Mary widow of David Luthemann, No Unit Given
Emily widow of George Cassell, No Unit Given
Rainer, Louis, 1 MO Eng
Muhlbach, Charles, 5 MO Cav
Schmidt, Franz, MO Militia
Heiling, Charles, 53 IL Inf

Brook, James, MO Militia
Maiton, Alfred, MO Militia
Maria widow of Christian V. Wald_ium, 2 IL Art.
Kassel, John, 1 MO Eng
Fanell, Thomas, 23 MO Inf
Sullivan, Timothy, MO Militia
Augustson, Cloedt , Captain, 119 NY Volunteers
Headricks, Louis, 56 Mass. Vols.
Barker, Barnhardt, Corporal, US Reserve Corps
Elvira J. widow of Wm. McIntosh, 6 Iowa Cav
Madilda widow of Duff, No Unit Given
Pruit, Oscar, No Unit Given
Hoffman, D. L., No Unit Given
Josephine widow of William Warner, East. MO Militia
Columie J. widow of L. F. Randolph, 2 IL Art
Yeager, Adolph , Sergeant, Cape Girardeau Home Guard
Kruger, Christian , Cape Girardeau Home Guard
Elizabeth M. widow of A. Kraft, Cape Girardeau Home Guard
Kattie M. widow of A. B. Carroll, Major, Cape Girardeau Home Guard
Wilhelmina widow of Henry Margraf, Cape Girardeau Home Guard
Lane, John, No Unit given
Ruth widow of A. H. O'Donohoue, No Unit Given
Williams, David, MO Militia
Peittreck, Jacob, Cape Girardeau Home guard
Rasterling, Frederick, MO Militia
Rabich, Henry, No Unit Given
Amalia widow of Sebastian Kage, No Unit given
Lane, Reuben (Col'd), 68 MO Inf
Hall, James E., 56 MO Cav
Ruessler, Frederick, 2 MO Inf
Slassaleuassan (Slaffullassun), Henry, 2 Iowa Art
Norton, Richard C., 42 OH Inf
Kempe, Conrad, 2 MO Art
Kage, F. A., No Unit Given
Mefford, George W., 7 KY Cav
Rachael widow of Sch____verge, MO Home Guard
Elizabeth widow of A. Puar, Cape Girardeau Home Guard
Hart, Benjamin (Col'd), 30 Iowa Inf.
Malinda widow of Samuel Williams, No Unit Given
Schrader, Frederick, 1 MO Eng
Charles, Jo____M., Cape Girardeau US Reserve Corps
Judice, Russell, MO Militia
Tuchmann, _____, No Unit given
Rabeck, Julius, 2 MO Inf.

Wills, Shelby (Col'd), Sailor
Heinze, Henry L., 2 MO Inf.
Ferdinan widow of John P_____, Cape Girardeau US Reserve Corps
Susan G. Gibb former widow of Joseph Gelos, 130 IL Inf.
Gocket, Auton, Cape Girardeau US Reserve Corps
Stephen, Conrad, Cape Girardeau US Reserve Corps
Smith, Henry A., 2 OH Inf.
Partels, Henry, Cape Girardeau US Reserve Corps
Martha M. widow of Whitaker, No Unit Given
Jeffords, Henry, 48 ILL Inf.
Koeber, Henry, MO Militia
Krueger, Goatlieb, No Unit Given
Louisa widow of Frederick Aug. Schwindler, 5 MO Art
Gregory, James, No Unit Given
Hopper, Henry C., 1 MO Eng.
Gertner, John W., MO Militia
Phelps, Henry C., 14 IL Inf.
Osterloh, Ernest, 56 MO
Mary Sloan widow of _____ Sloan, No Unit Given
Garonski, John Sr., 50 MO
James Powel, MO Inf. (Confederate)
Joseph Owens, MO Cav (Confederate)
Jackson McKinney, 56 MO Inf.
George W. Ripple, 15 IN Lt. Art
William C. Mizelle, MO Cav (Confederate)
William Stalhern, 8 MO Cav (Confederate)
Sidney Woldridge, 13 KY Cav
Ebenezer Welliford, 10 MO Cav, 2 MO Cav
James W. Young, 5 MO Inf. (Confederate)
Dudley Riennels, 29 MO Inf.
Mary R. widow of Wm. B. Ellsworth, LT, 1 IN Cav
John Kesterson, 50 MO Inf.
Henry A. Walker, 2 MO Cav
Elam McLand, 8 MO Cav (Confederate)
William Edmund, 13 IL Cav
Benjamin Under, 50 MO Inf.
Katharine widow of James H. Garner, MO
David Morgan, 7 Ark Inf. (Confederate)
Ignatz Vorrer, 6 MO Inf.
Austin L. Leeds, 73 IL Inf.
Dennis F. Cecil, 15 Kan (Ken) Cav
Henry Schinemann, MO
Hiram Richardson, 59 IL Cav
Elijah Clinginsmith, 56 MO Cav
John McCriee, Ark Inf. (Confederate
John Stanley, 3 W. VA Cav
Jacob S. Kirby, Mississippi (Confederate)
George P. Nations, 130 IL Inf.

William Bishop, 2 Ark Cav
James Ackerman, 7 KY Cav
Henry M. Craft, MO Cav (Confederate)
George McAne (McCriee), MO Cav
William E. Foster, No Unit Info (Confederate)
Fountain Blankenship, 13 KY Cav
Beck, Charles, 2 IL Art
Katharine widow of Joseph Kaiser, 149 IL Vol.
Johnson, Richold, 2 MO State Militia Cav
Hunter, Charles, 29 US Cd
Jackson, Davis, 118 US Col. Vol Inf.
Johnson, John, 60 US Col. Troops
Ische, Louis, 8 MO Inf.
Taubert, F. L, 5 MO Inf., 41 MO Inf.
Peter, Ezra, 95 OH Vol. Inf.
Schaefer, George, MO Home Guard
Ballinger, Michael, MO Home Guard
Bittlingen, Michael, 5 IL Lt. Art
Sch_lbt___, William, 12 MO
Kaupt, John, Benton Co. Home Guard, 2 MO Lt. Art
Fisher, John, 1 MO Eng.
Fisher, George, MO Militia
Hea_ing, Herman, 53 MO Militia
Engel___, Edward D., MO Home Guard
Field, Fritz, No Unit Given
Schrader, Deiderick, 8 E. MO Militia, 6 E. MO Militia
____gardh, Henry, MO Home guard, 2 IL Lt. Art
Carolina widow of Charles Molder, 13 IL Cav
Henslauer, John, 5 MO State Militia
Brickoff, Fritz, 1 MO Eng., MO Home Guard
Brinkhorst, John, MO Home Guard, 1 MO Eng.
Brineke, Frederick, 2 MO State Militia
Bock, Conrad, 2 IL Lt. Arty
Cassieneau, Louis, MO Home Guard
Araythen, Aug., 2 IL Lt. Art
Birde, Charles, MO Home guard
Bruening, Frederick, MO Home Guard, 1 MO Eng.
Galusha, Calvin B., 1 Wisc. Cav
Schrinson, Andrew, 12 MO Cav
Schleuter, Julian, MO Home Guard
Louise widow of Francis Friehlenghaus, MO Home Guard
Boch, Christian, MO Home Guard, 1 MO Eng.
_____ widow of Ernest Hundesteuerh, 2 IL LT Art
Houton, William, MO Home Guard
Walther, August, MO Home Guard
Jones, Jessee M., 132 IN Vol.
Willeke, William, 1 MO Eng., MO Home Guard
Trerrzistru widow of John Wittinor, 3 MO Cav
Cooler, Philip C., MO Home Guard, 3 MO Cav, 11 MO Cav
Thiesson, Henry, 5 MO Cav

Haupt, William, MO Home Guard
Schrader, Christoph, 1 MO Eng.
Daninger, Henry, MO Home Guard
Burwirth, August, 29 MO Inf.
Laudermann, Frederick, 12 MO State Militia, MO Home Guard
Heinz, August, 1 MO Eng.
Schl_cker, Guslat, 29 MO Inf.
Ulrich, Ernst, MO Home Guard, 1 MO Eng.
Steinmeyer, Christ, MO Home Guard
Schaefer, Michael, 4 MO Cav
Papp, John, 50 MO Inf.
Waelecke, William, 15 IL Cav, MO Home Guard
Asetholz, Henry A., 5 MO Cav
Kappel, Theodore, 56 E. MO Militia
Regenhardt, William, MO Home Guard
Heinze, Henry, 1 MO Eng.
Freederick, John, MO Home Guard
Sackmann, Daniel W., 5 MO Cav, MO Home Guard
Wilhelmine widow of Charles W. Sackmann, 15 IL Cav
Caroline widow of Frederick Wollier, 1 MO Eng.
Fassold, John, 1 MO Eng.
Schleuker, Gustave, 29 MO Inf.
Mary Vasterling formerly widow of Henry Heanschieal (sp) MO Home guard
Burwirth, August, 3 MO Inf.
Mayer, Fritz, MO Home guard
Bloomer, Samuel, 29 MO Vol.
Bergemann, William, MO Home Guard, 8 Prov. East MO. State Militia
Vasterling, Henry, 8 Prov. East MO Militia
Schultz, Charles, 1st Brigade Band 2nd Div 15 US Corps
Bleckworst, William, MO State Militia
Wittmor, Frederick, 18 IL Inf.
Brundis, Henry, MO Home Guard
Pullan, Richard, 65 US C Inf.
Amalia formerly widow of August Turnappell, MO Home guard
Johanna widow of Julius Vasterling, MO Home Guard
Nenninger, Henry, 2 IL Lt. Art
Nieschwitz, Adam, 2 IL Lt. Art, MO Home Guard
Hoern, Jacob, MO Home Guard
Christine, formerly widow of Christoph Schudenberg 2 IL Lt. Art
Maag, Philip, 4 MO Inf., 1 MO Reserve Corps, 2 MO Lt. Art
Gloth, Henry J., 12 MO Inf.
Pott, Frederick, 2 IL Lt. Art
Sauder, John N., 2 IL Lt. Art

Fastabend, Casper, MO Home Guard
Stein, Christian, MO Home Guard
Guthmann, Bernhard, MO Home Guard
Anna widow of William Oberheide, MO Vol. Cav
Meyer, Heinry, 1 MO Eng.
Caroline widow of William Ruppert, 2 Mich. Cav
Naman, Henry, MO Home Guard
Herbert, Michel, 1 MO Eng.
Pape, Christian, 5 MO State Militia, MO Home Guard
Bartmann, John, MO Home Guard
Bode, Charles, 8 MO Inf.
Ritgeroh, Christian, MO Home Guard, 1 MO Eng.
Penn, William J., 39 MO State Militia
William Henderson, US Soldier
Fritz Danes, US Soldier
Mahala Swan widow of George Swan, 65 US Col. Vol.
Isaac Coates, 12 PA Inf., 101 PA Inf.
Jacob H. Luttmann, 1 MO Eng.
Frank Munerstall, 2 MO Inf., MO Home Guard
William Obst, Muritocks Regt
Peter Ginries, 29 MO Inf.
Ignatz Goetz, 2 MO Lt. Art, MO Home Guard
Alexander Ross, No Unit given
Christian H. Krueger, 8 MO Inf.
Mike Zapf, 17 MO Inf.
Levi Garther, 56 US Col. Inf.
Amelia Thoshaner widow of William Thoshaner, MO Home Guard
Miller Kelley, 10 IL Cav
Rudolph Kluher, 56 MO
Emilie Harting widow of Christian Harting, 1 MO Eng.
Claiborn Bryant, 1 MO Eng.
Maryan G. Walker widow, US Sol.
Jane Holmes widow, US Sol.
Anton Southoff, US Sol.
John Vogt, US Sol.
Heinry Ulrich, 2 MO Inf.
John Watters, 1 IL Lt. Art
Christoph Stolte, 1 MO Eng.
Christian Klages, 8 MO, Home Guard Battalion
William Franke, 1 MO Eng., MO Home Guard
Frederick Miller, Home Guard Battalion, Cape Girardeau Battalion MO
Alexander Hall, 40 IL Inf.
Derick Z. (J.) McKan, 134 IL Inf, 135 IL Inf
Henry Arneling, 1 MO Eng
Haintah Van Frank widow of Lewis C. Van Frank, 2 IL Lt. Art
Anna N. Brunig widow of Ludwig Bruenig, 1 MO Eng

Anna Klingerman widow of Deidrich Klingerman, Cape Girardeau Home Guard
Mary Etsel widow of ReMaj John Herr, MO Home Guard
Christian Witcel widow of William Witcel, 1 MO Eng
Henry C. Baehre, 2 MO Lt. Art
Gottfried Garris, 1 MO Eng
Frederich Ross Kamp, MO Home Guard
Frederich Davis, Cape Girardeau County Guard Battalion MO
Joseph Frank, Cape Girardeau County Home Guard Battalion
Henry Meystedt, 30 MO Inf
Elizabeth Garris widow of Christian Garris, MO Home Guard
Conrad Gastocher, MO Home Guard Battalion
Lisette Dick widow of August Dick, 17 MO Inf
Andrew Geran, 1 MO Inf
Joseph Amstead, MO Militia
George Frinzel, Independent Militia MO
Christian Bainnann (Sp), MO Home Guard
Elizabeth widow of John Roth, remarried, MO Home Guard
William Schatz, MO Home Guard Battalion
Theirea Brown widow of Lewis Brown, 1 MO Lt. Art
George Hirsch, 22 IN Inf
Henry Lindemann, MO Home Guard
Frederick Weisenstein, MO Home Guard
Henry Voss, 29 MO Inf
John Reiker, MO Home Guard
George W. Travis, 79 Ohio Inf
Henry Nusbaum, 2 MO Vol.
Mary M. Herold widow of Valentine Herold, 2 IL Lt. Art
Nickles Heinzelmann, 2 IL Lt, Art
Matilda Salle widow of Otto Selle, 2 IL Lt. Art
Ferdinand Less, 56 MO
Alexander Williams alias Alexander Holland, 55 US Col. Inf.
Harriet Ivers widow of Smith Ivers, 56 US Col. Inf.
Hampton, George alias Hampton, Wade, 47 Miss Inf.
Kollus, Henry, MO Home Guards
Bohusuck, Ernest, W., E. MO Militia
Savers, Ruben, 21 MO Col. Inf.
Gayle, John, 2 MO Lt. Art
Sandross, Friedrich, 1 MO Eng
Ourich, Michael, 10 MO Cav, MO Home Guard Cav.
Eggimann, Benedicht, MO Home Guard
Matilda Eggimann formerly widow of Borchers, Henry MO Home Guard
Davis, Daniel, 26 KY Inf.

Sarah F. Dunsome widow of Tacket, William, 110 IL Inf.
Wilhelmina widow of Maevers, Christian, 8 MO Inf.
Wichlerick, Nicholas, MO Home Guard
Giborney, Dennis, 56 US Col. Inf.
Oster, G., No Unit Given
Celia A. widow of Hale, No Unit Given
O'Brien, Charles alias Obrian, Charles
O'Donoghue, No Unit Given
Mary A. widow of Carbol, No Unit Given
Eliza Jane widow of Houts, Christopher B., No Unit Given
Nancy J. widow of Athenton, No Unit Given
Mary A. widow of Roberts, Major Confederate, No Unit Given
Franz, Franz, MO Home Guard
Wilhelmina widow of Roettjan, John, MO Home Guard
Cofen, Thomas, 52 KY Inf.
Vogt, George, 24 IL Inf.
Jones, James W., MO Militia
Barben, Robert W., 56 MO
Carroll, Richard, 2 MO Inf., 15 MO Inf.
Kellerer, Anton, MO Home Guard
Pott, Henry A, 1 IL Lt. Art
Johanna widow of Frederick Pott, 2 IL Lt. Art
Henning, Adolph, 2 Kan Inf.
Wilhelmina Lose formerly widow of Wille, Frederick   MO Home Guard
Miller, Louis W., 2 IL Lt. Art
Feamer, James T., 12 KY
Francis A. widow of Wray, Joseph L., 15 IL Cav
Stratmann, John H., MO Home Guard
Heinze, Charles F., 15 IL Cav
Slaughter, James R., 29 MO Inf.
Baden, William, 2 MO Inf.
Henriette Heinze formerly widow of Henry T. Allers   MO Home Guard
Randal, Noah, No Unit Given
Goetz, Jacob, MO Home Guard
Margaret widow of Liebenkotter, John, MO Home Guard
Hogard, John L., No Unit Given
Woods, William E., MO Home Guard
Campbell, James T. alias James Campbell, LT., 15 IL Cav
Klostermann, Louis F., LT, 29 MO Inf.
Wells, John A, No Unit Given
Norvoski, Mathias M., 1 Wisc. Cav
Catherine B. widow of Christian Hirsch, MO Home Guard
Sarah J. widow of Berry, No Unit Given
Langlois, John, MO Home Guard
Landlois, Felix, MO Home Guard

Mary M. widow of David L. Meyers, MO Home Guard
Cofen, Nathaniel L., 10 MO Cav
Barbara widow of Girsch, Peter, MO Home Guard
Hartzell, James N., 7 Ohio Vol.
Wilhelmina widow of Roettjen, John, Canlled MO Militia, (duplicate records)
Elija A. Sledge, No Unit Given
George W. Bahn, No Unit Given
John Andrew Mcclain, 56 MO
Charles Clark, 43 Ind Inf.
Robert Nebl, 1 MO
John Joble, 4 MO
Lenbert, Bolk, 2 IL
John Minz, 1 MO
Joseph Ollford, 165 IL
William Ellis, 29 MO
Henry Floyd, 2 AR
Widow of John Sparlenger, 2 IL
Henry Kock, 1 IL
John W. Black, 13 MO
James Barton, No Unit Given
William P. Mcmillan, 2 MO
Jacob Friedrich, 4 MO
Washington Giboney, 102 Mich
William Dietler, 20 Wisc
Patrick Boyley (Bayley), 2 MO
Frederick Vornweg, MO Home Guard
John H. Jones, 2 MO
Ann Harrison widow of John Shepperd, 102 Mich
Richard Wilson, No Unit Given
Job Foster, Annie Foster widow, No Unit Given
Martin V. Speak,   No Units Given
    Lo—e, W. L. & John Cottner, John Jones Café, Richard Thompson
Maria c. Semper widow of John Sempler, 2 MO
James Bloomfield, 2 MO
Harris Kiibls, Confederate, No Unit Given
Freaser, John F., 3 MO Cav
John Eggemann, 1 MO Lt. Art
Dave S. Wan, 2 MO Inf.
August Hessell, 1 MO Eng
Lydia Fraser widow, US Sol.
Frederich Denecke, 5 MO Cav
August Bomemann, 5 MO Cav
Henry ___ralle, 5 MO Cav
Benjamin Melton, No Unit Given
William Northdurft, 5 MO Cav
Thomas B. Klm_1, Cav
Andrew H. Schlueter, Cav
Henry P. Ahrnes, 5 MO Cav
William Neiman, 5 MO Cav, E. MO Militia
William Illers, 5 MO Cav, E. MO Militia
Henry C. Schrader, 5 NY (KY) Cav

John Kerstner, 29 Ind Inf.
William Nienstdt, 5 MO Cav
William Fluge, 5 MO Cav
Louis Knap, No Unit Given
Henry Wessel, U.S.S.
William H. Winkler, U.S.S.
Charles Bartles, U.S.S.
William H. Willa, U.S.S.
Mary A. widow of Benjamin F. Mills, 13 KY Cav
Iorice widow of Isah Poe, Confederate, Cav
George R. Wilson, 55 Ind Inf., 132 Ind Inf., 12 Ind Inf.
Thomas J. McBride, 56 IL Inf.
William Ob—nt---, 21 IL Inf.
Henry C. Fraspen, 50 MO Inf.
Truman M. Ogde, 52 Ind Inf.
Harrison Couts, This man's family can't furnish info.
Charles Cauley, This man's comments come from informants
Henry Shaver, No Unit Given
Sandy F. Payne, No Unit Given
John Zirm, 1 MO Inf., 3 MO Inf.
Mandeville, Confederate, 2 Virginia Cav
L. L. Rosbury, Confederate, Cav
Henry F. Ohle-hlengen, 2 IL Art
Sarah C. widow of Hiram P. Crawfords, 32 Ind Inf.
Sarah E. widow of Frederick Brasa, 5 MO Cav
C-lesta widow of John H. Brasa, 2 MO Cav
Patrick Oharr (Ohare), 47 NY Inf.
Hiram Harley, 58 Ind Inf.
Henry C. Hinton, 8 MO Cav
Sarah A. widow of John McKee, Colored Regt
Absalom P. Kinden, Confederate, 8 MO
Charles Daume, No Unit Given
August Daume, 4 MO Cav
Henry Keehne, MO Inf
Henry Brase, MO Inf
Carolina widow of Christian Brakebusch, MO Cav
Alfred M. Hue-slep, MO Cav
Henry Eggemann, 1 MO Eng
Haarori M. Williams, No Unit Given
Deliverance Nichols, 1 MO Cav, 12 MO Cav
Edward Meegg, 8 MO, E. MO Militia
Charles Gartung, 5 MO Cav
Darah former widow of Henry Wilke, 2 IL Art
Mary widow of Columbus W. Bease, Confederate, Cav
Mary A. former widow of William Schinebin, 12 MO St. Cav
August Gue-hen, 3 MO State Militia Cav
Thomas Spivey, 2 MO Art
Robbert Thornton, 79 US Col. Inf.

Benjamin M. Mills, US Sol (duplicate)
Isaac Clark, US Sol.
Elizabeth Widigarrd widow, US Sol.
John M. Mabrey, 56 MO
Eliot Kinler, 56 MO Cav
Doeton F. Youngblood, 1 Ark Cav
Frederick Young, 3 MO Cav
Zera T. Summers, 4 MO Inf.
Christian Sperling, 2 IL Art
Frederick Anfal---, 29 MO Inf.
Jacob Crader, 50 MO Inf.
James Davis, 2 MO Art
William K. Piaffen, 56 MO Cav
John Link, 56 MO Inf.
Jacob Deck, Confederate, 8 MO Cav
Elisha F. Oldham, Confederate, 8 Mo Cav
Mary widow of Emery Ball, No Unit Given
John McLively, 92 IL Inf.
George W. Perst, Confederate, No Unit Given
Winfield G. Burford, 2 MO Art
Nicholas W. Slinkard, 56 MO Cav
George H. Bidnecke, No Unit Given
Wm. G. Thompson, Confederate, No Unit Given
August Bemekle, US Sol. No Unit Given
Thomas N. Hampton, US Sol. No Unit Given
Jesse Hartle, US Sol. No Unit Given
William C. Hayner, US Sol. No Unit Given
Gloth, William, 10 MO Cav
Christian Grebe, 1 MO Inf.
Thomas Slaughter, 3 MO Cav
William B. Eakens, 8 MO Cav, MO State Militia
Brookenbaugh, Henderson, 29 MO Inf.
Harmon Roloff, 65 NY Inf.
George H. Stephens, 6 MO Cav, MO State Militia
Ephraim Bell, 13 IL Cav
William O. Criswell, MO Cav
Samuel M. Mcanally, 6 IL Cav
Manerve E. Kinden widow of Davit G. Proffer, 2 MO Art
LeeAnna S. widow of Henry B. Sans, 22 Ohio Inf.
Henders C. Isbell , 29 MO Inf.
Samuel E. Stewart (Slewart), MO Inf.
LeeAnna P. widow of Virgal A. Prince, 2 MO Cav
William S. Hitchcock, Confederate, 8 MO Cav
Lewis G. Tapp, 10 IL Cav
Tarance Brady, Confederate, 5 TN Inf.
William R. Mathis, 5 IL Cav
William Hice, 1 Ohio Art
Henry Kestner, 29 MO Inf.
John Schatte, 58 IL Inf.
Patric Quinn, 29 MO Inf.
Jacob Rubbe, 1 MO Eng.
Henry Turncard, 1 MO Eng.

Anthony Gerchwiler, 1 MO Eng.
Thomas M. Haney, 10 MO Cav
Henry Martin, 1 MO Eng.
Hannah H. widow of Jurdon Mcombs, No Unit Given
Louis Schweltmann, 1 MO Eng.
William Schweltmann, 1 MO Eng.
Thomas B. Freeman, 29 MO Inf.
Frederic Hahn, 1 MO Eng.
Eliga M. Comstock, 40 IL Inf.
Hiram Simans, 9 NY Cav
Ellon B. widow of James W. Banran, No Unit Given
Brown, John M., 75 IL Cav
Foiste, William, 29 MO Inf.
Scism, Simear , 2 MO Cav
Rh---, Louis, 19 US Inf.
Tenier, Frederick, 1 MO Eng.
Kirchlofe, Henry W, 1 MO Eng.
Foister, Christian , MO Inf.
Kimmick, Benhard, 49 MO, 30 MO
Fritze, Louis, 1 MO Eng.
Kilkinson, James, 29 MO Inf.
Stugen, Leo J., Surgeon, No Unit Given
Schenider, Ernie, 1 MO Eng.
Stoll, Frederiche formerly widow of Frederick Hubach, 15 IL Cav
Huber, Christance formerly widow of August Brickmanse, 8 MO Inf.
Ervin, Marshall, 56 MO State Militia
Stug, George, 3 IL Art
Rollins, John, 1 Ala Cav
Kelpe, Christian, 2 MO Inf.
Watters, Louis W., 8 MO Inf.
Berringer, Catherine widow of Adam Berringer, No Unit Given
Goodchild, Elijah, 108 US Inf.
VornKahl, Conrad, 1 MO Eng.
Smith, Luke, 18 US Inf.
Joseph Kersterson, U.S.S.
Eugene W. Poe, U.S.S.
Rech, Frederick, 2 MO Lt. Art
Avery, Andrew M., 56 MO
Markers, Charles E., Confederate, No Unit Given
Daughterty, Sidney, 29 MO Inf.
Woods, Rufus M., 56 MO
Martin, James S., 8 MO Inf.
Nancy E. McDowell wife of James McDowell, No Unit Given
Anderson, Daniel W., 29 MO Inf.
Terra----B. widow of Wm. Garner, 50 MO Inf.
Trickey, John F., 5 MO Cav
Pritz, Joseph, 29 MO Inf.
Wilson, Archable, A., No Unit Given
Rich, Anthony, 5 MO State Militia Cav

Reid, Royal, 4 E. MO Militia
Kasten, Charles, 2 MO Inf.
Hope, Thomas D., Confederate, No Unit Given
Litzelfelnar, Andrew, 4 E. MO Militia Cav
Ross, Zenar, Confederate, No Unit Given
Penrod, Levi, 6 IL Cav
Hoell, John, 29 MO Inf.
Ross, Jasper, Confederate, Ark Cav
Ross, James A., Confederate, 8 MO Cav
Cratz, Michael, 29 MO Inf.
Brechl, Frederick, 12 MO State Militia Cav
Bea-, Deaniel. B., Confederate, 5 __ Inf.
D-----,Newton M., _ Mo State Militia Inf.
Rose, Thomas R., 2 MO Inf.
Templeton, Elam S., 29 MO Inf.
Huff, Albert N., 50 MO Inf.
Zimmerman, Charles, 29 MO Inf.
Brown, Marcus R., 5 MO Cav
John L. Neff, 111 __
John M. Yancey, 50 __
William E. Miller, 25 Wisc.
Charlie Widger, 49 IL
James H. Wiltheton, Confederate, 11 Texas Cav
Tobias Schoell, 50 MO Inf., 8 MO Inf.
Gurge Reisen, 29 MO Inf.
Orlando, Luck, 27 Ohio, 49 Ohio
Amanda J. Shoutts widow, No Unit given
Carlton, George W., 47 MO Inf.
Nolen, Noah, 59 IL Inf.
McNeill, Archibald A., 128 IL Inf.
Brewington, Reuben, 1 TN Inf.
Haile, Lemon, MO Inf., 56 MO Inf.
Whitmore, George R., 22 NY Inf., 155 Ind. Inf.
Mary Sherif widow of Andrew Fay, Cape Girardeau County Homeguard
_ivert, Wesley, 11 MO Inf.
Neissenbum, Freiderich, 41 MO Inf.
Louisa Birkmann widow of Herman Obershelp, 5 MO Inf.
Nasler, Matilda P. widow of William F. Garrison, 21 Ind Inf., 70 Ind Inf.
Dunning, Sarah P. widow of Samuel C. Dunning, Inf.
Noble, Job, 7 Neb Col (cav)
Cafren, Thompson, 10 KY Inf., 12 MO State Militia Col
Parketon, William, Sailor & Private Albatross, 40 KY Inf.
Davis, Louis, 58 Ind Inf.
Scheible, Christian, __ IL Inf.
Fellbinger, Henry, 1 Neb Col.
Julia R. widow of Looney, Oliver P., No Unit Given
Columbia A. widow of Manning, William D., No Unit Given
Horn, John A., 49 MO Cav

Elizabeth widow of Stephen Presnell, 78 MO Inf.
Louisa C. widow of William R. Looney, 2 MO Art
James E. Buckhannon, 50 MO Inf.
Barten W. Talley, Confederate, Carter's Battalion
George H. Miller, 56 E. MO State Militia
Polly L. Barr widow of Daniel Winter, 2 MO Inf.
Julia E. Davis widow of John W. Davis, 2 MO Art
Frederich M. Davis, Malitia
Elizabeth widow of John Brown, No Unit Given
George W. Davidson, 2 MO Lt. Art
Hiram N. Cox, Confederate, 22 TN Inf.
Roland Cubb, Cav
George G. Harp, Confederate, No Unit Given
James B. Welker, 2 MO State Militia Cav
Frederick Schuete, 2 MO Art
Justice L. Denton, 85 Ind. Inf.
William B. Robens, 2 MO Lt. Art
Nicholas Amos, Confederate, 8 MO Cav
Mary widow of Wolfenskirchler, Henry, 1 MO Eng.
William Moore, No Unit Given
Henry Bowers, No Unit Given
Fanntarnpt, C------(Sp), No Unit Given
Rogeanah J. widow of Stevens, William, No Unit Given
Henry H. Welty, 2 MO Art
Aarion H. L-avenpont, 56 E. MO State Militia Cav
Richard B. Davis, No Unit Given
Charles L. Talley, Confederate, 4 MO Inf.
Henry Server, 56 MO Cav
Peter Moore, 56 MO Cav
Andrew Moore, 56 MO Cav
William Mantz, 56 MO Cav
Wilmina widow of Haupt, John C., 56 MO Cav
Marian Fulbright, Cav
Elisha Mayfield, Art
Jacob Masters, Inf.
James Yates, 5 E. MO State Militia
Allen Ates, Cav
Aaron W. Riehn, Cav
Nelson Strang, 21 Ohio Inf.
Johnathan Dalton, Confederate, No Unit Given
Mary A. widow of Charles M. Turner Confederate, Cav
Charles B. Stearnes, Cav
Joseph Neiswanger, Confederate, No Unit Given
Francis M. Hearth, Confederate, No Unit Given
Sophie Slinkard widow of George McCrary, No Unit Given
Peter Neiswanger, No Unit Given
Jefferson B. Estes, No Unit Given

John Lriend (Sp), 16 NY Cav
Ernest Rieman, Cav
Emanuel Heartle, No Unit Given
John J. Wilferth, 5 Mo Cav
Surelda Guimps widow of James, Louis, No Unit Given
Perien L. Summers, 2 MO Lt. Art
John Wilferth, No Unit Given
Sarah A. widow of Warner Dodd, No Unit Given
Rene C. Love, widow of Elisha P. Jacobs, 93 Ind. Inf.
James H. Miller, 56 MO Cav
William C. Leslie, No Unit Given
Daniel W. Henderson, Confederate, No Unit Given
Sarah J. widow of Welty, Daniel M., 2 MO Art
James T. Caldwell, Confederate, 1LT, 15 MO Cav

CARTER COUNTY MISSOURI

This information was transcribed from National Archives microfilm. Names are in the order as they were on the film. Abbreviations used include: Ark for Arkansas, IL for Illinois, IN for Indiana, Wisc for Wisconsin, MO for Missouri, Col for Colored, Eng for Engineer, Cav for Cavalry, Inf for Infantry, Lt for Light, Art for Artillery. Where No Unit Given means no unit was shown on microfilm. Where Soldier or US Sol used means that is the only information provided on the microfilm. Carter County had no Confederates show up on this enumeration by mistake or otherwise. There was also one sailor.

NAME/UNIT

Farris, Spivey D., 29 IL Inf
Barame, Peter D., 50 MO Inf
Ray, Henderson, 2 Col. Cav
Heath, Granville T., 11 KY Inf
Davis, Edward B, 10 __ Cav
Haskins, John C., 50 MO
Emirth, Wiley, 87 IL
Ludia widow of Harget, Hiram, 59 IL Inf
Grandstaff, William, 141 Ohio Inf
Emaline widow of Broadis, Albert, IL Eng
Janet widow of Rose, Edlin R., 17 IL Inf
Haskins, Oliver G., 50 MO Inf
Marie Buchanin widow, No Unit Given
Lawrence W. Hubbersm, Soldier
John L. Green, 6 MO Cav
Charley S. Deinham, 77 NY Inf
Wiley Smith, 87 IL Inf
Benjamin F. Welch, 3 Ohio Cav, 25 IL Inf
James N. Jordan, 14 IL Cav, 1 IL Cav
Daniel H. Biddlecum, 19 IL Inf
James A. Galbreath, 18 Ohio Art
Aylett R. Crofton, 79 IN Inf
Daniel Austine, 14 IL Cav
John D. Stewart, 16 IN Inf, 5 IN Cav
John A. Kite, 12 MO Cav
Jubilee J. Posey, 31 IL Inf
John W. Staggs, 58 IL Inf
George W. Hardy, 6 IN Inf, 146 IN Inf
James M. Mathews, 7 Iowa Cav
Benjamin F. Butts, 6 MO Cav
Orlando C. Harvey, 2 MO Lt. Art
Eliza E. McKee widow of Michael McKee, 80 MO Inf
Albert Hill, 3 MO Cav
George J. Freeman, 37 IL Inf
Andrew J. Freeman, 2 NC Inf
Hiram A. Sharp, 1 Ark Inf
Alexander C. Harris, 2 IN Cav
John Fetngle, MO
William H. Main, 58 IN Inf
Margaret E. widow of William O. Turley, 11 MO Cav
Anthony Toursend, 99 IL Inf
John Jaco, 5 MO Cav

Henry Schupp, 5 IL Cav
David S. Gatewood, 68 MO Cav
David Kirkpatrick, 17 Ohio Inf
Laurence Fox, 22 IN Art
William Jones, 11 MO Cav
Abigal widow of William J. Barns, 2 Col Cav
Barbary Moran former widow of Perry Peyton, 183 Ohio Inf
James Weaver, 30 IL Inf
Wm. N. Larkin, No Unit Given, US Sol.
Richard A. Jones, No Unit Given, US Sol.
James H. Tyler, No Unit Given, US Sol.
Thomas Mangers, No Unit Given, US Sol.
John W. Dunn, No Unit Given, US Sol.
James Green, Capt. Shaddock's Regiment
Marian Rogers, 31 MO, 47 MO
Thomas Hause, 2 MO Cav
George Gresham, 136 IL
James Hill, No Unit Given
John Smith, 3 MO Cav
Lebi H. Harvey, 11 IL Inf
Henry Tucker, 60 MO Militia
Francis Sherrer, 6 MO Cav
A.P. Rose, 15 MO Inf
Silas Sanders, 9 IL Cav
Isaac Roymer, 47 MO Inf
Miles Roymer, 3 MO Inf, 2 US Inf
David Cock, 51 IN Inf
James Leach, 31 MO Inf
Jacob Angle, 50 MO Cav
Thomas L. Faris, 2 MO Cav
Jesse Robertson, 4 MO Cav
Andrew J. Secrease, 31 MO Inf, 32 MO Inf
Lydia Harder widow, No Unit Given
Jonah Crouch, Michigan Inf
Nathaniel Pace, 5 MO Cav
James W. McDonald, 124 IL Inf
Joseph Pice, 24 IN Inf
James Fuller, No Unit Given
Charles H. Hearin, 7 Kan Cav
Louis Delcoure, 13 MO Vol.
Nathan R. Jetmore, No Unit Given
John R. Smith, 6 MO Cav
James M. Allred, No Unit Given
William Cox, No Unit Given
Els Smith, 50 MO
James A. Hill, No Unit Given
J. E. Wood, No Unit Given
Samuel Luker, No Unit Given
Aldarina Gosnell, No Unit Given
James Smallwood, No Unit Given
Elizabeth Smart widow, No Unit Given
Adaline Toliver widow, No Unit Given
Wm. F. Horning, No Unit Given
Hiram Berry, No Unit Given
Thos. A. House, No Unit Given
J. A. Rives, 50 MO Inf

Harriet Baker widow of George W. Baker, No Unit Given
Andrew Luck, 50 MO Vols.
Mary A. Benning widow of Christopher Benning, 52 IN Inf
Margret A. Rook widow of Chester C. Rook, No Unit Given
S. L. Dunnigan, 5 MO Vol.
Humphrey Garris, 3 MO
Geo. J. Jordan, 57 IL Inf
Owen Caffrey, No Unit given
C. C. Russel, 13 Wisc Cav
Robert McCallister, No Unit Given
William Hunter, No Unit Given
Chesterfield Carey, No Unit Given, US Sol.
Hiram Cook, No Unit Given, US Sol.
Jesse Bowerman, No Unit Given, US Sol.
John Odom, No Unit Given, US Sol.
John W. Williams, No Unit Given, US Sol.
August Falk, No Unit Given, US Sol.
James W. Smith, No Unit Given, US Sol.
William Reed, Corporal/Sailor, 40 NJ/USS House
Samuel P. Hampton, 47 MO
Reason F. Leslie, 33 IL, 1 Ark Cav
William N. McCain, MO Home Guard
William Walter, No Unit Given
John B. Maramurt, 50 IN
Arthur Parsons, 10 IN
John McCarty, 146 Ohio
James Hardcastle, No Unit Given
Jonas Hedrick, 146 Ohio
Benjamin Pinnard, No Unit Given, US Sol.

DUNKLIN COUNTY MISSOURI

Dunklin County had a lot of Confederates show up on this census. Names were lined out and Conf written in margin. I have indicated where a Confederate shows up by using word Confederate on name line. Standard Abbreviations used include: Inf for infantry, Cav for Cavalry, St. for State, MO for Missouri, IN for Indiana, IL for Illinois, Miss for Mississippi, Ala for Alabama, Flo for Florida, Kan for Kansas, KY for Kentucky, TN for Tennessee, Ark for Arkansas, Mich for Michigan, Neb for Nebraska, NY for New York, Lt. For Light, Art for Artillery, Mtd. For mounted, Wisc for Wisconsin, VA for Virginia, Geor for Georgia. No Unit Given indicates no unit was shown on microfilm. US Sol. Or soldier indicates that is all the information provided on the microfilm.

NAME/UNIT
George W. Hagle, 11 MO Inf
Alford M. Orr, 6 IL Cav, 68 IL Inf
John T. Crawford, 1 Ala Cav
Robert Perry, 16 IN Inf
Danford M. Rice, 5 MO Cav
Granville Young, 1 TN Cav
Jefferson Standridge, No Unit Given
Johnathan Gregory, Confederate, No Unit Given
John W. Byer, 29 Ohio Inf
James Ranic, 52 IN Inf
J----n Paschal widow of Jesse Paschal, 87 IL Mtd. Inf
Samantha Kellems widow of D. M. Killems, 66 IN Inf
Jacob Snider, 52 MO St. Militia
Benjamin F. Snider, 5 MO Cav
Jasper N. Weathers, 2 MO Cav
Mary A. Pennington widow of Elija Pennington, Sailor, USS Vermont
Adaline Palmer widow of Hiram Palmer, 49 IN Inf
Ferdinand Gehrig, 2 MO Cav
Jasper Vanmeler, 8 IN Inf, 31 IN Inf, 8 IN Cav
John M. Feeghner, 29 MO Inf
Richard W. Gunn, 87 IL Inf
Johnathan Gregory, 27 IN Inf
William D. Butts, 6 TN Cav
Rufus D. Place, 49 IL Inf
Isace Lorne, 48 KY Inf
Luther Place, 49 IL Inf
Hiram Gear, 12 MO Cav
Julia S. Hedspeth widow of _____Hedspeth, 6 TN Cav
_____Benson widow of _____, 42 IN Inf
Chism Lacy, 2 MO Militia
William E. Bray, 77 East MO Militia
James McCutcher, 1 Iowa Cav
William Atchley, 65 IL Inf
Stephen Mayfield, 56 MO Cav
Loranza D. Bowman, 13 IL Cav
_atasch Williams, Sailor, USS George Manning
John R. Mason, 7 US Inf
Francis M. Snider, 52 MO St. Militia Cav

John Williams, 1 IL Cav
John T. Cross, 61 Ohio Inf
Martha Crawford widow of Samuel A. Crawford, 1 Ala Cav
Mary J. Higginbotham widow of John Higginbotham, 52 MO Cav State Militia
John Q. A. Gardner, 1 Ala Cav
Sarah Dougherty widow of Jordan Dougherty, 12 IL Inf
Hannah Rice   widow, No Unit Given, US Sol.
Francis K. Harris   widow, No Unit Given, US Sol.
Rachael Harper   widow, No Unit Given, US Sol.
Jerry M. Thompson, No Unit Given, US Sol.
David J. Storm, 52 KY Mtd. Inf
Benjamin F. Liliker, Confederate, 10 TN Cav
William F. Blake, Confederate, 10 Ark Inf
Nancy A. widow of Abram Keanton, Confederate, Ark.
William C. Bird, Confederate, 12 KY Cav
Chas. McKinney, 111 IL Inf
Thomas Jackson, Confederate, TN Inf
Missouri J. widow of John E. Roberts, Confederate, 14 Miss Inf
Chaplin N. Merrill, Confederate, 8 KY
Mack Hayrs, Confederate, 10 TN Inf
John H. Loftis, Confederate, 38 Ala Inf
Carolina Bownears widow of Jacob Bownears, 12 Neb Cav
Elizabeth Higginbotham widow off Jasper Higginbotham, Confederate, MO
Robert McDaniel, No Unit Given
Erlderian E. Porche, 1 MO Inf
La_iriza Smith widow of Thomas _. Smith, 5 IN Inf
George W. Kirabrill, No Unit Given
Edo L. Widow of Pleasant Gordon, 16 IL Inf
Elizabeth widow of William R. Crain, 31 IL Inf
Samuel Ringold, 1 MO Lt. Art
Thomas M. Stanfill, 5 MO Cav
John Kitrel, 60 IL Inf
William J. Williams, 1 IL Art
William Irby, 56 IL Inf
John Smith, 16 KY Inf
Thomas Bradley, Confederate, 38 Ala Inf
John T. Summers, Confederate, 7 Kan Cav
James H. Carlile, 56 IL Inf
Daniel Doolen, Confederate, 32 MO Inf
Hannah E. widow of Thomas J. Hoosier, 7 TN Cav
Benjamin M. Huggins, 68 East Missouri Militia
Peter Barnett, 49 IL Inf
John W. Shaw, Confederate, 36 Flo Inf
Nancy Carson widow of John Carson, 75 IN Inf
George T. Copeland, Confederate, 11 MO Inf
Thomas _. Williams, 16 MO Inf
George W. Stone, 42 IN Inf
Thomas Baysinger, 50 MO Inf
Serald Fitzgerald , 15 MO Cav
James M. Corder , Confederate, 8 MO Inf
Joel B. McGinger, 6 IL Cav
Julia F. widow of F. M. Lutterel, Confederate, 18 Miss Cav
George D. Hatch , 7 TN Cav
Louis L. Loferney, Confederate, 15 MO Cav
Jesser____J. Knight, Confederate, 4 MO Lt. Art
Willis Snider, 12 MO Cav

James P. Haggard, 6 TN Cav
William H. Hampton, 7 TN Cav
John M. Lewis, Confederate, 12 MO Cav
Lydia widow of Andy Holtzhouse, 12 MO Inf
James H. Shones, Confederate, 13 Miss Inf
Manerva widow of John Ward, 16 Ark Cav
Clabern Blanton, Confederate, 3 Ark Inf
John L. Arnold, Confederate, 3 Miss Inf
John R. Anders, MO Inf
Henderson Irby, 9 Mtd. IL Inf
Thomas Casey, 5 Iowa Cav
Jane King widow of William King, 2 Ark
John Stewart, 1 MO Inf
William R. Speers, 9 KY Inf
Josiah W. Hammonds, MO Militia Cav
Damon Daniels, 14 KY Mtd. Inf
William H. Crain, 60 IL Inf
John B. Skidmore, 155 IL Inf
Eli M. Summers, Confederate, 16 TN Inf
Richard H. Vaughn, 10 TN Inf
Granville Fitzpatrick, Confederate, 28 Ark Inf
John P. Rich, Confederate, 8 TN Inf
William Darwell, 16 KY Inf
Arthur C. Gillett, 20 IL Inf
John Stephens, 60 IL Cav
Obediah Copeland, 40 IL Inf
William J. Harris, 13 Ark Inf
_____A. widow of George H. Brazell, 61 IL Inf
Rosimary widow of Charles Stillwell, 39 Wisc. Inf
Milton H. Stout, 12 Mich Inf
William P. Duncan, 128 IL Inf
James H. Leigh, Confederate, 3 KY Cav (could be Mtd. Inf)
Nancy widow of David Lisk, 2 Ark Cav
Alfred S. Watson, Confederate, 1 MO Cav
John H. Betts, Confederate, 47 TN Inf
Alden H. Spooner, 86 Ohio Inf
William H. Haut, Confederate, 4 TN Inf
William J. Stone, Confederate, No Unit Given
William R. Wethers, Confederate, 1 MO Cav
Victoria E. widow of James Ellegood, 130 IL Inf
Amanda widow of David Burns, Confederate, 34 MO Inf
Lizzie H. Jones wildow of William A. Jones, Confederate, No Unit Given
Henry Bohleke, 1 Wisc Cav
Lucinda widow of Henry Eppehemer, 14 IL Cav
William Bragenlong(Bragriulon), 116 IN Inf
George W. Proffer, MO Inf
Samuel D. Bates, 40 Iowa Inf
Johnson Malott, 1 Mich Cav
Grant A. Debow, Confederate, 33 TN Inf
Mary A. widow of Spiva A. Gossett, Confederate, 41 TN Inf
Charles B. Mrtcalfr, Confederate, No Unit Given
John H. Slaten, Confederate, No Unit Given
Martha widow of Washington Tefteler, Confederate, 8 TN Inf
John Dewitt, 87 IL Inf
William W. Nunley, No Unit given
Garrett Weaver, Confederate, 38 MO Inf

Richard Glover, 21 KY Inf
Robert C. Bolen, Confederate, 3 KY Cav (could be Mtd. Inf)
Charles Metzger, Wisconsin
Daniel Haynes, 18 IL Inf
Nathan S. Macheris, Confederate, 2 Miss, 33 Miss Inf
Hallett B. Spooner, 68 IL Inf
Thomas B. Reeves, Confederate, MO Inf
Robert C. Wade, Confederate, 8 Ark Cav
John Lane, Confederate, 124 Ala
Sarah P. Widow of George Goldenwirth, Confederate, 10 Geor Cav
Thomas J. Guthrie, IN Inf
Richard C. Proctor, 100 PA Inf
Richard H. McHaney, No Unit Given
Margaret widow of John Ashworth, Confederate, 64 KY
William M. Taylor, 12 KY Cav
Eliza J. widow of Thomas Gilmore, 24 Kan Cav
Thomas J. Gerstner (heavily lined through), Confederate, 10 TN Cav
Timothy M. Hosener, 47 NY Inf
Henry N. Phillips, Confederate, 18 MO Inf
Robert McCarver, 2 Ark Cav
Elizabeth widow of John C. Nite, 6 IL Cav
George M. D. Haslip, 2 MO Inf
Zacoriah N. Hall, 48 MO Inf
George S. Napper, 56 MO Militia
Isaac Potter, No Unit Given
Sarah L. widow of Wilson Leary, Wisc
John Thompson, 35 KY Inf
Mary A. Crawford former widow of John A. Stubbins, No Unit Given
Perry Dye, 8 TN Cav
Mary M. widow of Noah Medley, No Unit Given
Martha J. Babb former widow of George W. Binges, 7 TN Cav
Henry B. Hall, 59 IL Inf
Wiley McFarland, No Unit Given
Rufus Lynn, 17 KY Inf
Moss M. Rice, 143 IN Inf
Melvina W. widow of William Bailey, 13 Ohio
David McNatton, 8 Iowa
John Hall, Sailor
James H. Wilborn, 29 MO
John W. Wisely, 10 VA Cav
Rubin L. Crossnor, 18 IL Cav
Benjamin F. Todd, 3 MO Cav
John P. Todd, 33 MO Inf
Elija Lance, Soldier
Margaret widow of Andrew C. Bassham, 13 MO Cav
Luther, G. M., 29 IL Inf,
Taylor, A. M., 144 IL Inf
Gibson, J. T., 35 KY Inf, 17 KY Cav
Bodine, J. V., 1 Wisc Cav
Landrum, Henry, 16 KY Cav, 2 IL Cav, 13 MO Cav
Grimsby, J. D., 2 IL Cav, 13 MO Cav
Francis Ray former widow of Joseph Hargis, No Unit Given
Summers, J. C., 29 MO Inf
Branch, J. W., 31 IL Inf
Scales, W. H., 140 IN Inf
Carlie, A. J., 10 MO Cav

Elizabeth widow of L. V. Bird, KY Inf
Wayne, S. C., 86 IL Inf, 14 IL
Applecate, H. A., NY State Militia
Bolivre T. Seargrove, No Unit Given, US Sol
John M. Norris, 60 IL Inf
John W. Smith, Major Service Reserve Battalion
H. G. Ellis, 65 IL Inf
Numerian H. Kelly, 6 Iowa Cav
F. M. Miller, 30 IL Inf
James White, 7 Ala Cav
Lewis C. Graves, 2 IL Art
John W. Gibbs, 9 TN Cav
Charles Nerremes (Kerrimes), 19 Ohio
Manha J. Bidwell widow of Frank Bidwell, No Unit Given, Soldier
Savanna Richardson widow of _____ Richardson, No Unit Given, Soldier
S. Adline Barnes widow of _____, No Unit Given, Soldier
Mahaly Underwood widow of _____, No Unit Given, Soldier
Clara H. Wilson widow of _____, No Unit Given, Soldier
Nancy E. Ginn widow of _____, No Unit Given, Soldier
William H. Pool, 57 IL Inf
William Linsey, Miss Inf
John P. Marcund, 47 MO Inf
Arnold G. Roberds, 10 TN Cav, TN Inf
Isham P. Richardson, 16 Ala Inf (this was a Confederate Unit)
Joel Vaughn, MO Inf
Pheba Jones widow of Monroe Jones, IL Inf
James P. Gist, 2 TN Inf
John Cockrum, MO Inf
Benjamin Farmer, 45 TN Inf
William Harden, Confederate, Ark Inf
James Grigsby, Confederate, 19 Ala Inf
John Kriess, 6 TN Cav
John Frasier, Confederate, 9 TN Art
John Dunigan , Confederate, 66 NC Inf
William Bird, Confederate, 27 Ala Inf
William McCoy, 8 Ohio Inf
Andrew Gillpatrick, 144 IN Inf
William Patton, 2 TN Inf
Ruebin C. Marcum, No Unit Given, US Sol.
John Johnson, 91 IL Inf
Van M. Dempsey, 50 MO
Jessy _roper, 2 MO Inf
William J. Browner, 3 MO Cav
Is___ Clinton, 10 MO Cav
Benj C. Canon, No Unit Given
William Furi, Tyler US A Gunboat
A.M. Grace, 1 KY Cav
John B. Williams, 65 IN Inf
Daniel Callhan, 130 IL Inf
D. H. Williams, 65 IN Inf
John W. Black, 2 MO Art
John B. Hendricks, 2 TN Inf
John W. Long, 10 TN Inf
Charles Bassett, 144 IN Inf
Thomas W. Southland, 11 KY Cav
Jessey Lorance, 41 MO Inf

G. W. Monroe, 16 Kan Cav.
David Call, 9 TN Cav
Benney Killpatrick, No Unit Given
William H. Mathews, 20 TN Inf
William A. Stanfill, 5 MO Cav
John F. Wells, MO
George W. Quinn, 31 IL Inf
John R. Pool, 6 TN Cav

IRON COUNTY MO

Census records here use the following abbreviations: Inf for infantry, Cav for Cavalry, Mich for Michigan, Wisc. For Wisconsin, Mtd, for Mounted, Lt. for light, Art for Artillery, Col. For colored, Neb. for Nebraska, NY for New York, IL for Illinois, MO for Missouri, Ken for Kentucky, Ark for Arkansas, Vol for volunteer, Mass for Massachusetts, Penn for Pennsylvania, Provis for provisional, WVA for West Virginia, KY also for Kentucky, IN for Indiana, Eng for Engineer. Occasionally a Confederate's name appears, was then lined through by census taker with annotation Confed in left margin. I have indicated those who were Confederates after the names. All others listed are presumed to be Union soldiers.

NAME/UNIT

Williams, Joseph A., 5 TN Cav
Duncan, William, 31 Iowa Inf
Chapman, James A., 32 MO Inf
Copeland, Amrbose C., 7 TN Mtd. Inf
Miner, Laban E., 13 MO Cav
Bay, Green B. W., 48 MO Inf
Martha A. Hall widow of Thomas C. Hall, 10 MO Cav
Douglass, David W. E., 1 Neb Cav
Lucinda J. Sumpter widow of Franklin Sumpter, 1 MO Lt. Art
Strickland, James W., 3 MO Cav
Callahan, Thomas, 48 US Col. Inf
Adams, John R., 31 MO Inf
Mary A. Smith widow of Cullen O. Smith, 40 MO Inf
Ren—hausen, Henry I., Absent from house and no person could befound to provide necessary information
Eaton, Andrew H., 25 MO Inf
Dane, Leo H., 12 Ken Inf
Fortuer, George W., 3 MO Cav
Jane Fortuer widow of William H. Fortuer, 29 MO Inf
Cureton, David, 32 MO Inf
Martha widow of Hornbeck, Simpson, 2 MO
-racker, Andrew W., Body Guard, No Unit Given
Raradine A. widow of John Miller, 50 MO Inf
Alfred C. Crackin, Confederate, 28 TN Inf
Wesly Henderson, Confederate, 25 TN Inf
Peter Pauley, No Unit Given
George Williamson, 58 IN Inf
James M. Daurrand, MO Art
Henry Myers, 3 Vol Cav
William J. Sutton, 8 MO
Thomas Fortrane, 50 MO Inf

John S. Luthey, 83 IN Inf
William Grayson, 3 Iowa Cav
William Starvestine, Confederate, No Unit Given
Joel A. Griffit, 26 IN
Hughy Eaton, 3 MO State Militia Cav
Henry Wright, 3 MO State Militia Cav
Henry Rencehausen, could be duplicate, 1 Wisc. Cav
John T. Akers, 37 Ken Vol.
Syntha A. widow of Mitchel Delashunt, 10 MO Cav
Christian Muntner, No Unit Given
John W. Ragan, 32 MO
Henry Hoveris (Hovens), 36 Ohio
Smith, E. M., 34 Mass. Inf
Oesterly, Christian, 32 MO Inf
Kermet, Nathan C., 17 IL Cav
Shruner, Joseph, MO
Ranft, Joseph, 14 MO Cav
Sweeney, John C., 12 MO State Militia
Dermy, Jefferson, 3 MO State Militia
Koeth, Mary widow of Anthony Koeth, 29 IL Inf
Carver, George E., 22 Ohio Inf
Raple, John S., 2 NY Cav
Cunningham, Francis widow of Charles
Cunningham, 68 MO State Militia
Jackson, James W., 22 Ohio Inf
Mead, John C., 5 MO State Militia
Johnes, Jehu, 27 Ohio Inf
Obrien, Daniel, 12 MO Cav
Johnson, James K., 62 IL Inf
Hines, Jacob, 3 IN Vol.
Pele, Graft M., 54 Penn Vol.
Ruhl, Peter, 2 MO Vol.
Mund, Lewis, MO
Dunn, Margaret widow of _____,
    Cannot assertain

Kirchner, Catharine widow of Henry Hartman, No Unit Given
Rickman, John, 13 MO Cav
Daniel H. Hartman, 12 MO Cav
Elizabeth Thorp widow of Lewis C. Thorp, 17 Iowa Cav
Sarah Spencer widow of William Spencer, 6 MO Cav
Daniel Smith, 3 Iowa Cav
John Lashley, 91 Penn Cav
William Webb, 6 MO Cav
James W. Hedgcoth, Cav
Catherine widow of Ferdinand Scherrets, MO
Elizabeth Logan widow of _____, No Unit Given
Joseph Huff, 8Provis East MO Militia
Magdaline Rutschanan widow of William Scheidt, 2 MO Art
Isaac Barts, 13 Penn Cav
James H. Chase, Inf
Robert L. Lindsey, 1 MO Inf, 68 East MO Militia, 50 MO Vols.
Claybaugh, Martin L., 6 MO Inf
Kate Claybaugh widow of John _. Denby, 21 IL Inf
Hugh M. Bradley, 3 MO Cav, 47 MO Inf
Jacob T. Ake, 31 MO Inf
Eli D. Ake, 1 Iowa Art
Henry Rasche, 2 MO Inf
Mary Goodenough widow of Calvin Goodenough, 24 NY Inf
Henry L. Sunerman, 31 MO Cav
Sara M. Carlile widow of Alexander M. Carlile, 3 MO Cav
America C. Ligon widow of William H. Ligon, 3 MO Cav
Albert Voils, 115 IL Inf
Mary Ann Gay widow of Samuel T. Gay, 47 MO Inf
Perseus R. Crisp, 4 Iowa Inf
Fields Trammel, No Unit Given
Mary Grinson former widow of Frederich Osterly, 10 Ohio Inf
John Seff, 45 KY Inf
Catherine Woolem widow of Jacob Woolem, 8 MO Inf
Martin Raph, No Unit Given
Catherine Breslin widow of John Breslin, 2 MO Art
James Corde, 27 MO Inf
Mary Corbier widow of Charles Corbier, 6 MO Cav
James R. Highley, 8 MO
Mary Jenkin former widow of George Greer, Unable to get information

Susan F. Cotter former widow of Robert L. Cox, 11 IL Cav
Samuel Battle, 88 IL Inf
Henry Esterling, 1 MO Inf
Sarah Welsh widow of James Welsh, 2 MO Inf
Henry Henderson, WVA Cav
Charles Machmeyer, MO Home Guard battle of Pilot Knob
Mary Killalee widow of John Killalee, Couldn't get information
William Biel, Couldn't get information
Henrietta Dittmer widow of Frederich Dittmer, 6 MO Inf
Valentine Effenger, At battle of Pilot Knob
Fredericka J. Richter widow of Henry Richter, 2 MO Inf
Jacob Schaffer, 2 MO Inf
Frederich Kaths, Home Guard battle of Pilot Knob
Philip Kolb, 2 MO Inf
Samuel T. Dennison, Ship-Blackhawk
George Spitzmiller, Segers Art
Henrietta Elson former widow of Charles Koehler, MO Home Guard
Sarah P. Hampton former widow of Jackson Childers, 47 MO
Charles Immer, 49 MO
Peter Geatenmeyer, 49 MO
Chaterine Ripper former widow of Peter Boyer, 48 Penn
Henry Peitz, MO
August C. Gockle, MO
Lorenz Nehmer, MO Home Guard
John Schwab, 47 MO
Francis Wesnard, No Unit Given
Franz Dinger, 47 MO
William E. Jones, Couldn't get information
John Schmidt, No Unit Given
Elya B. Smith, 29 MO
John C. Barton, 34 Iowa Inf
Christopher C. Keathly, 39 KY Inf
Henry Elsman, MO Home Guard
William Backof, MO Home Guard
Amanda Gilliam former widow of John Brighton, Couldn't get information
Frederick Ficht, MO Home Guard
Charles Holliman, 65 MO
James E—les, Couldn't get information
Nancy Moon widow of _____ Moon, Couldn't get information
John Schwab Sr, 47 MO
Annie M. Brightstein widow of John Brightstein, Couldn't get information
Martin Wolfe, 5 MO Inf
Annie -. R-s-tie widow of Jacob Mitchel, 2 MO Lt. Art

Charles F. Morgan, 4 MO Cav
Frank Brickley, 2 MO
Henry Elsman, 5 MO
Burt Jones, 12 MO Cav
Sarah E. Voils widow, No Unit Given, US Sol.
Mary J. Riley   widow, No Unit Given, US Sol.
Caroline T. Heinichs widow, No Unit Given, US Sol.
Louis Mind, No Unit Given, US Sol.
Jasper M. Ossick, No Unit Given, US Sol.
Goulding, Yan R., 1 MO Cav
Lax, Moses, 62 MO
Hodge, Aronld, 47 MO Inf
Martha E. widow of Bice, George, 2 MO Inf
Elliott, Aaron, 21 IL Inf
Joseph, Hasty, 21 IL Inf
Fletcher, William A., 47 MO Inf
Martha A. widow of Ardinared, Augusts, No Unit Given
Albert, John, 22 IL Inf
Peck, Carroll R., MO Home Guard
Hill, Robert J., 34 IL Inf
Jane widow of Evens, David B., 1 Ark Inf
Hodges, James, 98 IL Inf
Greman, Russell, 91 IL Inf
Hogue, John A., Confederate, 5 MO Inf
Emerson, John W., 47 MO Inf
Leonard, Henry C., 24 NY Inf
Temperance widow of Personel, Thomas J., 32 Iowa Inf
Jones, Mary widow of Lewis, Zebulon, Minnesota Art
Martin, Azariak, 47 MO Inf
Campbell, James, 47 MO Inf
Mary Marshall widow of Marshall, Benjamin, 47 MO Inf
Strembaugh, James, 27 MO Inf
Boswell, Joshua, 33 Iowa Inf
Good, Solomon, 132 IN Inf
Guffy, Nelson P., 88 IN Inf
Collison, Richard, Confederate, 1 MO Inf
Sutton, William, 29 MO Inf
Casteel, William, 1 MO State Militia
Moore, Caloway, 24 MO Inf
Dettmer, Adolph, 2 MO Lt. Art
Young, George H., 8 MO Cav, 68 MO Cav
William H. N. Stiner, 31 MO Inf, MO Cav
Francis Benjamin, 31 MO Cav, 14 MO Cav
Susana Lofton widow of George Lofton, 144 IL Inf
John N. Thompson, 6 MO Cav
William N. Sutton, 24 MO Militia
Isaac Sutton, 24 MO Militia
Elenz W. Gault, 22 Wisc. Inf
William O. Savage, 29 MO Inf

David O. Markham, Indiana
James W. Wilson, 3 MO State Militia, 14 MO Cav
Benjamin F. Bone, 50 MO Inf
William B. Gillman, Sailor, ship-Vermont
Elias Heiff, 1 MO Cav
Carroll Smith, 50 MO Inf
William Bunce, 9 Mich
William S. Reed, 1 MO Eng.
William Binder, 18 IL Inf
Henry Midkiff, 2 MO Heavy Art
George W. Pinkney, 47 MO Inf
Chas. W. Ellis, Independent Co.
Evin Maynard, 6 TN Cav
Mary Burch former widow of Richard McAllister, 47 MO Inf
Caleb Ballared, 29 MO Inf
Andrew Meyrs, 51 MO Inf
M. Hays, 5 (Mus?) Inf
Thomas H. Howard, 47 MO Inf
Delphia Vaughn widow of Jeremiah Vaughn, 9 MO Inf
James Reed, 47 MO Inf
Aaron Mead (lined through—no explanation given)
Gottlieb, Frank (lined through—no explanation given)
Joseph Bubb, 6 Kansas
Van Dunnigan, 6 MO Cav
John McFadden, 14 MO
Charlie M. Talley, 13 IL Cav
James M. Huston, 16 IN Inf
John B. Hampton, 47 MO Inf
James Scheldin, 3 Wisc. Inf
Mary Robinson widow of Valentine Robinson, 2 MO Inf
Elizabeth Jackson widow of Thomas Jackson, 47 MO Inf
Charles Hurt, 10 MO Inf
Royert Reynolds, 33 IN Inf
Martha Reynolds widow of William Harris, 47 MO Inf
Riley Harris, Inf
Edwin May, 99 IL
Martha Alexander widow of Rufus Alexander, No Info
Augustus Lolz (Lotz), 69 Ohio Inf
Delaney Night alias Phillip L. Night, 4 Ark
John Middleton, 50 MO
Enoch De Board, No Unit given
C. C. Russell, 2 Ark Cav
Louis D. (P.) Austin, 14 IL Cav
Frank R. Raney, MO Inf
John M. Kelly, 2 Ark Cav
John Hall, 22 Ohio Inf

Joseph M. Stevenson, widow Catherine, 12 MO Cav
H. _. Lucy, 53 TN Inf
B.F. Russell, 2 Ark Cav
Andy McCluie (McLure), 68 MO Cav
Wm. C. Jones (James), 68 MO Cav
B.F. Meadows, widow Louise Meadows, 5 MO Cav
Y.V. Obannon, 8 MO Cav
George W. Toppins, 5 MO
Cyrus J. Victory, 11 MO Inf
William Willet, 6 MO Cav
James Hughes, 50 IL Inf
Franklin Hall, 21 NY Inf
Milton Clifton, 68 MO Cav
Rebeca Young widow of David Young, 29 MO Inf
Rufus Kensick, Vandalia (?)
Barney McCul, 3 TN Cav
Milton Radford, 47 MO Inf
J. W. Stevenson, 47 MO Inf
John Crowley, 29 MO
Jerry Berryman, 3 MO Cav
Thomas Farrer, 32 MO Inf
James Johnson, 47 MO Inf
Edwin Tarr, 47 MO Inf
William Mcguire, No Unit Given, Sol. US
Cassander Horton (lined through), Sol. US (1812)
Aaron Meard, No Unit Given, Sol. US
Benj. Mackey. No Unit Given, Sol. US
Robert W. Woody, No Unit Given, Sol. US
Cyrus Lawson, No Unit Given, Sol. US
Marcellus Cole, No Unit Given, Sol. US
Littleton Vickery, No Unit Given, Sol. US
William C. Harmon, No Unit Given, Sol. US
Martha Francis widow, No Unit Given, Sol. US
Thomas Henderson, No Unit Given, Sol. US
John Long, No Unit Given, Sol. US
Catharine Allen widow, No Unit Given, Sol. US
Isaac Hill, No Unit Given, Sol. US
George N. Sawyer, 10 IL Inf
Samuel Robinson, 8 MO Inf
Jacob Brewer, 47 MO Cav
Argus Cowan, 3 MO Cav

MADISON COUNTY MO

Census record abbreviations include: Ark for Arkansas, IL for Illinois, IN for Indiana, Ind for Indiana, KY for Kentucky, Ken for Kentucky, TN for Tennessee, Tenn for Tennessee, PA for Pennsylvania, Penn for Pennsylvania, Inf for infantry, Cav for Cavalry, Lt for light, Art for Artillery, Col for colored, Vol for volunteer, LA for Louisiana, Miss for Mississippi, Wisc. For Wisconsin, MS for Mississippi, Del for Delaware, MO for Missouri, Neb for Nebraska, Sol for soldier, Mich for Michigan, US S for US Soldier, Vet for Veteran.

Occasionally the census taker would record soldier's name or widow's name before finding out Confederate—line drawn through entry and Conf in left margin. I have used Confederate on name line. All others are presumed to be Union soldiers.

NAME/UNIT

The names below appeared mixed in with Bollinger County MO:
Morris, Louis W., 80 Ohio
Slinkard, Peter, 5 MO Inf

The names listed below were in the Madison Co. MO census:
Rufus Baird, Confederate, MO Inf
Felix G. Gregory, Confederate, 2 MO Cav
Elisha Richardson, No Unit Given
James Smith, 1 MO Cav
Bennett M. Wimer, 10 MO Inf
Ancil Matthews, Confederate, 10 MO Inf
John Santhoff, 7 IL Inf
Jacob M. Rhodes, 47 MO Inf
Henry Walden, 49 US Vols
William Nifong, Confederate, No Unit Given
John C. Ramey, Confederate, 5 TN Inf
Cynthia E. Cromer widow, No Unit Given
Richard Brooks, 50 MO Inf
Horace D. Benedict, 3 Ohio
Rabecca E. McQuary widow of Robert C. McQuary, No Unit Given
Frank May, 21 Penn Cav
Reuben Albert, 111 IL Inf
Frank Shulte, 50 MO Vol.
Aaron A. Butts, Confederate, 7 LA Vol.
Teresa M. widow of Amos J. Bruce, No Unit Given
Laura widow of Henry J. Fox, No Unit Given
Francis Simino, 15 IL Cav
William E. Shearer, 101 IN Vol.
Daniel L. Glaves, Confederate, 3 KY Inf
John C. Spivac, Confederate, 3 MO Inf
Benjamin McGraw, Confederate, 24 Miss.
Isac N. Turnemire, 14 KY Vol.
William M. Wilson, 8 MO Vol.
Jeremiah Tatem, 14 Penn Cav
Finas B. Stephens, 47 MO Cav
Andrew F. Ruth, 1 MO Art
Joseph Lacvaub, No Unit Given
John F. Burns, Confederate, No Unit Given
Letitia H. Beasley widow of Thomas A. Beasley, Ark Inf
Richard Devin, 30 Kan Inf
John W. Wray, 50 MO Inf
Albert G. Black, 47 MO Inf
Henry R. White , Confederate, No Unit Given
Robert B. Gray, 2mate, ship—Lizzie Southard
Rebecca A. Matthews widow of Jeremiah Matthews Confederate, No Unit Given
Sarah L. Obanon widow of Daniel W. Obanon Confederate, No Unit Given
Lizzie Hicks widow of George M. Hicks Confederate   No Unit Given
Bernard O'Connor, 11 US Army
Josephine Bamber widow of Levi E. Bamber, No Unit Given
William H. Phillips, 12 Ohio Inf
Jasper Belkner, 68 MO Inf
William Holladay, Confederate, 3 MO Cav
Malissa A. Scott widow of G. W. Scott, 10 MO Cav
Smith, John O., 3 MO Cav State Militia
Abbey, Edward T., 2 IL Lt. Art
Joseph J. McDowell, 30 MO
William H. Adams, No Unit Given
Rudolph Riner, 50 Wisc.
John Tucker, 50 MO
Wilson Thompson, 50 MO

Henry J. Rehkop, 2 MO Art
Mary C. Cole widow of Ira B. Cole, No Unit Given
James P. Whiteaker (Whileaker), 3 MO
Philip J. Schulte, 47 MO Inf
John Sunderman, 47 MO (MS) Inf
Micheal Thompson, 7 MO Cav
Hermann Kaths, State Militia
John Ranes, Confederate, MO
Michael Hasller, No Unit Given
James J. Holley, 50 Vrle (I have no idea what this is), but Could be 50 MO Vols.
John Johnson, State Militia
Frederick Maberry, 47 MO
Samuel Johnson 47 MO
James B. Richardson (lined through), Mexican War, 1 TN Vols.
William O. Hart, 30 MO
Samuel H. Olanin, 2 MO State Militia
John Sarnint, 6 MO
Joseph W. Alexander, No Unit Given
Marshall P. Cayce, No Unit Given
James W. Williams, No Unit Given
Martha Byres widow of Goodman Byres, Confederate, No Unit Given
Henry Bave, Confederate, 2 MO Cav
William Bray, Confederate, Whts. Mat.
Peter Smith, Confederate, 3 TN
Thomas Underwood, 47 MO Inf
Abram Umfleet, 11 MO Inf
James Leigh, Confederate, 5 Ala Cav
Fritz Knolbhoff, 12 MO State Militia
James A. Tuckler, No Unit Given
Charles C. Ashbaugh, 122 IL Inf
Levi Bess, No Unit Given
Josiah Hood, 47 MO Inf
Isreal L. Hahn, 5 MO State Militia
Winfield S. LaGrand, 50 Penn
James Welch, 50 MO Inf
Joseph D. Wilson, 2 MO Lt. Art
James T. Howell, No Unit Given
Charles Robinson, No Unit Given
Samuel McGee, No Unit Given
John C. Howell, 8 TN Cav
Moses Thomas, Confederate, 3 MO Cav
Thomas H. Harn, Confederate, Shelby's brigade Elliss Regiment
William P. DeGuire, Confederate, M.L. Clandy's unit
Francis Semins, 3 IL Cav
William Newberry, MO Cav
Benjamin P. Cahoon, 1 Del Inf
Madison M. Walker, 136 IL
William W. Kell, No Unit Given
Mary widow of Thomas Yancy, 6 IL Inf
William H. Copass, 36 Ohio Inf
Harrison Fulton, No Unit Given
Nancy W. widow of Handers Wilson, Confederate, No Unit Given
John Umfleet, 50 MO Inf
John Blake, 18 IL Inf
Sarah Morris widow of Willis Morris, Confederate, No Unit Given
Emily DeBlois widow of Peter DeBlois, Confederate, No Unit Given
James G. Donnell, Rains Div
Henry Trussell, 6 MO Inf
Henry Seahse, 30 MO Inf
John Nichols, No Unit Given
Reuben Lamar, Confederate, No Unit Given
Ruth Wonsy widow of Samuel H. Clark, Confederate, 3rd Mimms Battery (could be Mississippi)
Hiram Berry, 3 MO Cav
Erastus H. Day, 2 PA Heavy Art
Isaac N. Ramsey, No Unit Given
Randolph Z. Vaughn, Capt. Brewer's Co.
Daniel (David) Wilson, No Unit Given
Came Steward, Confederate, No Unit Given
Sarah E. Sands widow of Jehu Rosecrans, No Unit Given
Thomas Semp, No Unit Given
James M. Berryman, Confederate, General Taylor's
George W. Kinney, Confederate, 1 KY Cav
John H. Bess, 79 MO St. Militia
John B. DeBlois, No Unit Given
Moses Cayce, No Unit Given
William J. Edwards, 47 MO
James F. Henderson, Cousnist (I have no idea what this is)
William Holley, No Unit Given
Andrew J. Hahn, 47 MO Inf
William J. Curl, 4 Conf (Could be Consolidated) TN
James Rosselot, 7 Ohio Cav
John J. Hahn, 47 MO Inf
Jacob Karsch, V(U)RC (could be US Reserve Corps)
Joseph Burdeth, Confederate, No Unit Given
Zachariah T. Picker, 13 MO Cav
Alspazarah Kennedy widow of William C. Kennedy Confederate No Unit Given
Martin V. Pator, 6 Penn Cav
Henry Jones, Confederate, No Unit Given
Mary A. Lunsford widow of Isiah W. Lunsford Confederate, 3 MO Cav
Elizah Peterson widow of Daniel Peterson Confederate, 3 MO Cav
Elizabeth Polite widow of Philip Polite, 47 MO Inf

Margaret Duvall widow of Thomas Duvall Confederate, No Unit Given
Luther E. Jenkins , Confederate, 8 MO Cav
Sertimus W. Chilton, Confederate, 2 MO Cav
Henry M. Spray, No Unit Given, US Sol.
Allen W. Fisher, No Unit Given, US Sol.
Benjamin Lachance, No Unit Given, US Sol.
John Hermes, No Unit Given, US Sol.
Hardon Williams, No Unit Given, US Sol.
Joseph Ballinger, No Unit Given, US Sol.
Susan E. Millis (Willis) widow, No Unit Given, US Sol. Widow
Mary J. Walson (Watson) widow, No Unit Given, US Sol. Widow
Joseph Gower, No Unit Given, US Sol.
Rose Grant widow, No Unit Given, US Sol. Widow
Frank Ballinger, No Unit Given, US Sol.
Albert Romando, No Unit Given, US Sol.
Mary Yancey widow, No Unit Given, US Sol. Widow
Jonathan Williams, No Unit Given, US Sol.
Skaggs, Edward, 50 MO Inf
White, John, 50 MO Inf
Berry, William P., 50 MO Inf
Joel Hall, 22 Iowa Inf
Day, Mills P., 1 KY Inf
Counts, Williams, 50 MO Inf
Harris, Fielding D., 40 MO Inf
Shaw, Joshua, 3 MO Cav
Shults, George W., 48 MO Cav
Woods, William, 3 MO Cav
Baldwin, Vasdy, 50 MO Inf
White, William H., 50 MO Inf
Turnese, Charles K., 3 MO State Militia Cav
Brookes, Benjamin F., 50 MO Inf
Murray, Elizabeth widow of A. J. Murray, 50 MO Inf
Harris, James H., 45 KY Inf, 4 KY Inf
Cornles, Fielding R., 50 MO Inf
White, Luke L., 50 MO Inf
Underwood, David E., 48 MO Inf
Underwood, George W., 3 MO State Militia Cav
Underwood, Ephraim, 47 MO Inf
Manning, James T., 5 MO Cav
Shelton, John B., No Unit Given
Ward, George N., 2 Tenn Cav
Betzel, Julius A. , 5 MO State Militia Cav
Kainnainger, Frederick, No Unit Given
Rhodes, King D., 12 MO Cav, 3 MO Cav
Ragan, Henry P., 50 MO Inf
Frances E. King widow of Thomas J. King, 27 MO Inf
Dowd, Marcus, 6 Mich Cav
Narrew, Ossan A., 6 Mich Cav
Clay, John A., 13 MO Cav

Pierce, Francis M., 14 MO Cav
Brown, _. K. P., 6 Tenn Inf
Watts, Robert, 50 MO Inf
Delany, Charles, 29 MO Inf
Higdon, James T., 3 MO State Militia Cav
Saukford, Charles T, 26 IL Inf
Arthur, David, No Unit Given
Shrum, Frederick S., No Unit Given
Higdon, William H., 1 Col Cav, 5 Col. Cav
David Bollinger, No Unit Given
Nancy Berry, No Unit Given
Sarah A. Clutcher widow of John F. Clutcher, No Unit Given
Elija Whiteur, Confederate, illegible
James J. Whiteur, Confederate, Marmatthus C. army
George C. Whiteur, Confederate, No Unit Given
John F. Bess, Confederate, MO
Barbary Bess widow of Levi Bess, No Unit Given
Isaac Murray, No Unit Given
Racna E. Jordan, 15 KY
Mahala M. Baster widow of Levi Baster, 2 MO
Thomas Batter, 2 MO
Sidney Colter, 2 MO
Francis M. Nelnson, Confederate, Artillery
Wm. C. McHenry, IL Lt. Art
McCardin C. Davis, No Unit Given
Carline Davis former widow of Marin B. Messer, Art
Carlin Sityes widow of Abram F. Whiteur, No Unit Given
Eli S. Sityes, 68 MO Militia
John A. Gocher, Confederate, 34 NC
Alford _. Carver, 79 MO
Thomas S. Prithy, Confederate, Jeffrey's Regt.
Geo. W. Dellinger, Cannot find any information
Roda Carltan widow of L___. Carltan, Cannot find any p—tenloss
Jas. H. Stanfill, 79 MO
Jacob Lutes, Confederate, Cav
Elizabeth Watson widow of Joseph Watson, 9 Reg't IL
Orlander J. Penince(sp?), No Unit Given
Jacita Rhodes, 3 MO
Robert W. Ragsdale, No Unit Given
David F. Ragsdale, 5 Reg. MO
William W. Sutherland, 9 MO State Militia
Ben F. Fruger, No Unit Given
John F. Mowser, Confederate,No Unit Given
Josiah E. Mowser, No Unit Given
James M. Cooke, No Unit Given
Miles Mowser, 10 Mis (could be MO)
George Cook, 47 MO
Annie widow of Wm. M. Robins, No Unit Given

Susan A. widow of Ransom Rhodes, No Unit Given
King H. Recker, US S
Christian Rhods, US S
Richard R. Johnson, US S
John W. Burkes, US S
William F. Stephens, 47 MO Inf
Henry F. Krueller, Confederate, 7 MO
John M. James, illegible
William B. Anthony, Confederate, 8 MO
John W. McKelvey, 1 Ohio
William M. Coat (could be Cook), 17 KY
George W. Skagg, Confederate, No Unit Given
John W. Tinnin, 3 MO State Militia
Malim Yount, Confederate, 3 MO (Price's Army)
Albert Bess, Confederate, 7 MO
Benjamin M. Piefler, 13 MO Vet
David Farquhar, 137 IL Inf
Ahrru J. Beardsley, 1 Ark
James F. Paul, 2 Iowa Cav
Ira Morris, No Unit Given
Thomas L. Brasswell, 13 KY
Jane widow of Toppin, No Unit Given
Jessee F. Innman, 47 MO Inf
John Woodmansee, 6 MO Cav
August Rinnpf, 1 Neb Cav
James M. Henry, 5 V(U) R. C. Inf
Peter Wise, No Unit Given
Harrison Rose, No Unit Given
Francis Meagher, No Unit Given
Thomas J. Smith, No Unit Given
Allen Francie, 68 MO
William Miller, 47 MO
Peter Henry, 33 MO Inf
George W. Mathews, 6 MO Cav
James Casteel, 67 IN Inf
Francis L. Mattinger, 47 MO Inf
Jeremiah Rion, 117 IL Inf
Harvey P. Nenuker, 4 PA Cav
Frelding T. King, 6 MO Inf
James Hirst, 13 IL Cav
Martha E. Henson, widow, No Unit Given, Sol. US
Kinser, Christopher, No Unit Given, Sol. US
John Reeves, No Unit Given
Danial J. Rusal, 2 Ark Cav
Mary C. Nuckles widow of ___. W. Nuckles, 47 MO Inf
James H. White, 47 MO Inf
(illegible), 47 MO Inf
Noomey M. Heley widow of Bartley M. Heley, 3 MO State Militia
Miles H. Stacey, Confederate, No Unit Given
Joseph Simpeson, 2 Tenn Cav
William M—rey, 3 MO Cav
Jas. Strombought, 29 MO Inf
Calvin Grahan, 68 East MO Militia
George Dav—hive, 31 IN Inf
E. A. Wilkinson, 47 MO Inf
John A. Hipes, 148 IN Inf
Whitney Sevall, 97 Ohio Cav
D. (P.) M. C. Smith, 50 MO Cav
Pleas. Golden, No Unit Given
Rice Dawnhen, 11 MO Inf
J. M. Green, 8 MO Cav
James M. Ross, (shows)Confederate, 1 Ohio Cav
Elizabeth Fowler, No Unit Given
Jugo D. McWilliams, 67 IN Inf
Joseph Johnson, 50 MO
James M. Johnson, 50 MO
Burrell G. Burks, 29 MO
Alfred Rhodes, 2 MO Lt. Art
William M. Cravat, 47 MO Inf
Mary C. Whittenberg widow of Andrus A. Lowrance, 31 MO Inf
Charles Sumner, 91 IN Inf
Henry F. Pruett, 6 MO Cav
Crawfo-t H. Pruett, 6 MO Cav
William Watts, 47 MO Inf
Albert E. Davis, 66 IN Inf
America S. Rutherford widow, No Unit Given US Sol

MISSISSIPPI COUNTY MISSOURI

Standard abbreviations used include the following: MO for Missouri, NY for New York, Ill for Illinois, Ind for Indiana, Me for Maine, MA or Mass for Massachusetts, Inf for infantry, cav for cavalry, art for artillery, TN or Tenn for Tennessee, KY or Ken for Kentucky, Ark for Arkansas, PA for Pennsylvania, (Col) or Col for colored, sol for soldier, LA for Louisiana, Miss for Mississippi, VA for Virginia, Wisc. For Wisconsin, Lt for light, vol for volunteer, and Mich for Michigan, Regt for Regiment.

Confederate is shown although in most cases these entries were lined through when the census taker realized the individual or widow was Confederate. This was a Union Veteran's census.

NAME/UNIT or ship

Thomas J. Dalton, Jeffreys' Regt
William P. Hedge, No Unit Given
Presley Rhodes, Confederate, No Unit Given
Alfred R. Thompkins, 16 NY
Joseph Mortphart, 14 Me (MA)
Miles E. Burris, 163 Ill (Iowa, Indiana) Inf
John H. Bolen, Confederate, 5 TN Inf
Demarias Holland widow of Jerymire Holland, No Unit Given
Jerssey West, 49 Ill
James H. Tall, Confederate, 1 MO Cav
James H. Hanley, 7 Georgia (Confederate maybe)
Adaline Malone widow of J. M. Malone, Ill Cav
Edward C. Rean, 37 Ill Inf, 1 MO
Geo. A. Soloman, 4 TN Inf
Henry H. Pierce, Cinnatus (Sp?, don't know what this means)
Delphia A. Ashcraft former widow of A. C. Milliner, 50 MO
George W. Brown, 11 KY
Julia H. Grigsby wife of Aron T. Grigsby, No Unit Given
Lenard Tall, 68 MO Col.
Frank Higgins, 65 Ill Vol.
Sam Sims, 4 Col. Heavy Art
Henry Sneed, Gun Boat Te_rton
Alex Beckwith, 4 Col. Heavy Art
Micheal T. Hagin, 5 MO Cav
Henry Shepherd, 31 PA Cav
Terressa Gebbare widow of John Gebbare, 5 MO Cav
Senylar I. Hawkins, 9 KY Cav
Mattie Crenshaw wife of late RoberT. G. Smith, 36 Ill Inf, 6 Il Cav
Dudley Ervin, Illegible
Calvin Freeman, 49 Col Inf
Henry Fisher, No Unit Given
Jerry Brown, No Unit Given

Spencer Rivers, 9 Col. Troops
Leonyd G. Frehcn, 9 KY Cav
Charles Scott, No Unit Given
Alex Mabry, U.S. Sol.
John Esery, U.S.Sol.
Henry Williams, U.S. Sol
Waid Boyd, U.S. Sol
Joseph Isaac, U.S. Sol
Louisa C. widow of Jewell Jasepers, 25 Ohio Inf
Woodfolk, Alexander, 12 US Art
Elizabeth widow of McAllister, Ponss, 4 KY Art
McElmurry, Richard, 68 MO Inf
Slack, Charles M., 111 Ill Inf
Hinton, Jethro, 2 TN Cav
Rowe, John M., 7 TN Cav
Parker, Henry H., 6 Ill Cav
Mary V. widow of Hobbs, John K., 14 MO Cav
Frie, Jonathan, Seaman, ship—Mound City
Barlow, Charles, 14 Ill Inf
Parisker, William H., 130 Ill Inf
Laura Loflin formerly widow of Rerves, Jerome B., 31 Ind. Inf
Young, Archibald, 48 KY Inf
LaMontague, Louis, 12 Ind Cav
Richard Thomas allias Moreman, Dick, 123 US Col. Inf
Sandridge, Green, 73 LA Inf
Pruett, Valentine, 1 MO Cav
Lynn. William P., 15 KY Cav
Jones, Robert H., 72 Ohio Inf
Snelling, William H., 4 KY Cav
Adams, Zachery T., 1 KY Inf
Cook, William J., 37 KY Inf
Mary A. Hobson formerly widow of Busby, Sheppard 56 Ill Inf
Forbes, Thomas B., 89 Ind Inf
Buckner, David P., 31 Ill Inf
Hall, William, 29 Ill Inf
Ridger, George W., 50 MO Inf
Lynn, Samuel H., 15 KY Cav
Bond, John W., 56 Ill Inf

Eaves, Andrew J., 30 KY Inf
Snodgrass, Elija, Marine, ship—Mound City
Hall, David, 29 Ill Inf
Davis, Telightly widow of John Davis, 29 Ill Inf
Kane, Malindy widow of Kane, Thomas J., 29 Ill Inf
Thomas, Peter, 68 MO Inf
Davidson, John, 56 Ill Inf
Bartlett, Stanley, Soldier
Samuel W. Irwin, Soldier
Harvey Clifford, Soldier
Levir Max, 77 Ohio Inf
Charles L. Crail, 36 Ohio Inf
George W. Stewart, 4 MO Inf
Simon McCernurry, 68 MO Inf
James Jackson, 61 MO Inf
Jacob _. Goodin, No Unit Given
James Rodgers, 11 MO Cav
Joseph Moore, 8 KY Inf
Atlas B. Fisher, 6 Ind Inf
Robbert Black, 4 KY Inf
James Devat, 10 US Col
Joe E. Meareman, 8 MO Inf
Peter Lee, 11 Ill Inf
James P. Withrow, 24 Ind Inf
Simon B. Rothchild, 11 KY Cav
William A. Porterwood, 29 Ill Inf
Randolph M. Harper, 120 Ind Inf
George W. Reagan, 23 MO Inf
John Bearnit (Blarnit), 56 Ark Inf
Louis Thomson, 56 Ark Inf
James B. Bibb, 7 Ark Inf
Hiram Cuffay, 15 Ohio Cav
Charles B. Valandingham, Illegible
Mary A. Martin formerly soldier's widow, No Unit Given
Bell Valandingham formerly soldier's widow, No Unit Given
Laura Rooney, No Unit Given
John P. Lawrence, 3 Wisc. Inf
Catherine Harter former widow of Eliga Hurten Confederate (Ill Inf. ?)
Marton, Boils, Confederate, 4 TN Inf
George T. Carter, Confederate, 20 Miss Inf
John Henry, 15 Wisc. Inf
John Melody, 69 Ill Inf
Thomas Braxton, Confederate, 42 Miss Inf
John H. Manly, Confederate, 19 VA Cav
Comfort B. Forgery widow of Robert B. Forgery, MO Cav
_____ D. Harris, Confederate, 7 TN Cav
Thomas Fulkerson, 81 Ind Inf
Mary F. Strater widow of James McFarlin, No Unit Given
James S. Swank, Confederate, 6 MO Cav
Erdin J. Rowls, Confederate, 1 TN Lt. Art

Senepta Cobb widow of Simon E. Cobb, TN Cav
Delilia Nuvals widow of James Nuvals, MO
Elizie J. Parker widow of Thomas Parker, Ill
John D. Murphy, Confederate, 3 MO State Guard
William White, Confederate, No Unit Given
Sarah Kerton widow of Procktor Kerton, 131 Ill Inf
Shencer Mathis, 7 TN Cav
Francis Cole former widow of Morris Carrell, TN Cav
John A. Hastings, 3 KY Cav
Joseph Lee, 22 Ind Inf
Samuel Bowlin, 101 Tenn Inf
Katie Bowlin former widow of Eliga Mason, 122 Tenn Inf
Margaret Pettis formerly widow of Jerry Walker (Col) US TN INF
Roberts, Amos (Col.), 4 US Heavy Art
Linder, William, 23 Ohio Inf
Annie Arner, formerly widow of Hickman, John (Col.) No Unit Given
Goliah Beckwith alias Chambers, William (Col.), 29 US Inf
Russell, William M., 17 Ohio Vol. Inf, 6 Ohio Vol Cav
Margaret Lucas widow of Isaac Lucas (Col), KY Inf
Williams, Edmund (Col), Art
Emma Lucas formerly widow of Bumpus, Henry (Col) No Unit Given
Pursell, J. W., 25 Ind Inf
Sally Jones widow of James Jones, Inf
Tom Jones, VA
Patsy Barton formerly widow of Herron, John (Col), Gunboat--Conestoga
Jane Austin, formerly widow of Carr, Henry (Col), 4 US Heavy Art
Bowden, Jerry (Col), 4 US Heavy Art
Wade, Charles (Col), 4 US Heavy Art
Burlington, Geo. M., 63 Ohio Inf
Combs, Abram D., 42 Ind Inf
McElmury, Thomas (Col), 4 US Heavy Art
Kate Hunter, formerly widow of Buldock, George (Col), 4 US Heavy Art
Martha J. Lewis widow of Lewis, Start, TN Inf, KY Cav
Johnson, Prince (Col), 8 Heavy US Art
Melvina Davis, formerly widow of Rowe, Geo. W., No Unit Given
Wright, Amos, 28 KY Cav
Douglas, John (Col), 16 Army Corps, the Pioneer Corps
Johnson, Elbert D., 29 Ill Inf
Young, James M., 11 KY Inf, 17 KY Cav
Clinton, James (Col), No Unit Given

Mollie Webb widow of Webb, Ezekiel (Col), 2 US Col Troops
Rebecca Hale, formerly widow of Hartsfield, William, KY Cav
Taylor, Anderson (Col), 4 Heavy Art
Lemon, John, 6 Mich Cav
Ackley, John W., 86 Ohio Inf
Swope, James G., 4 Ind Battery
Pettigrew, Caleb (Col), 3 US Col. Heavy Art
Mary Besheares widow of Besheares, Givry, No Unit Given
Susan ridley widow of Riddle, Henry (Col), 4 US HeavyArt
Ella Bates, widow of Bates, John D. (Col), No Unit Given
Ella Bates formerly widow of Musgrove, James (Col), No Unit Given
Burlingame, Edward P., 1 Ohio Vol. Cav
Crotty, John, ship—Union; ship—Massachusetts
Wesbrook, Jacob (Col), 4 US Heavy Art
Eddna Cuff, widow, Soldier
Albert Tally, Sol (US)
Albert Ferguson, Sol (US)
Wilson, G. M., 47 Ind Inf
Mary widow of Lane, Samuel, 1 Tenn Cav
Martha E. widow of Colvin, James L., MO Cav
Walter, _entrorn J., 30 KY Inf
Moore, William T., Navy, ship Silvos, Lake No. 2
Pettigorue, William, 3 Heavy Art
Martha widow of Rhodes, John R., 131 Ill Inf
Hawkins, William L., 8 TN Cav
Luther, Willis, 4 Heavy Art
Combs, William P., No Unit Given
Dusow, Anderson, 4 Heavy Art.
Pettigorue, Wesley, No Unit Given
Turner, Gravy widow of Turner, James, 4 Heavy Art
James, M. James, 10 Tenn Inf
Leonard, Samuel J, 101 Ill Inf
Cain, Joshua M., 34 Ind Inf
Dickson, Philip F., 51 LA Inf
Griffin, Samuel, 8 US Heavy Art
Thompson, William, 38 NY Inf
Cotton, Armstead, 8 Ill Inf
Clark, Elely widow of Turner, Turner, 4 Heavy Art
Johnson, Laura widow of Johnson, Frank, 4 Heavy Art
Elizabeth Brown, widow US S
Mary Adkins, widow US S
Robert Holton, US S
Alice C. Leonard, widow US S
Collins, Hugh A. , Confederate, 3 KY
Wilson, John M., 145 Ill
Branham, Hiram, 14 KY

Haley, Gree F., 18 Ill
Fergueson, Brice, 8 Ill
Bankston, George, Confederate, 2 Ark
Grace, James D., 50 MO
Martha J. Drake widow, Confederate, cannot answer questions
Hortin (Hastin), Samuel J. B., 9 Ill
John H. (W.) Bras_ee, 12 Ken
Farnsworth, Jackson, 10 Ill
Hall, L. (H.) Alfred, Confederate, 3 MO
Nancy E. Pearson widow, US   No Unit Given
William Higgins, Sol. US No Unit Given
Delana Kellams, Sol. US No Unit Given
William Gregg, Sol. US No Unit Given
Wood, William R, 81 Ind Inf
Rose, Pleasant, No Unit Given
Graff, John R., No Unit Given
Boid, Walter A., 30 KY Inf
Fowler, William H., 10 Mich Cav
Shelley, Isaac D., No Unit Given
Lowery, Elias, 50 MO Inf
Bradley, Elijah F., 6 Ill Cav
Raben, Josiah, 50 MO Inf
Marshal, Martin V. B., 11 Ill Inf
Eastwood, James, 18 Ill Inf
Berry, Samuel E., 29 Ill Inf
White, James G., 6 Ill Cav
Shelley, Joseph, 50 MO Inf
George M. Trife, 184 NY Inf
Short, Joshua, 48 Ill
Cutting, George, 20 __ Inf
Wright, Eliga, 54 Ill Inf
J.R. Drew, No Unit Given
Elisa Adams, widow US
Saley Chambers, widow US
William H. Hubbell, US Soldier
George Austin, US Soldier
Martha C. Childers, widow US
William I. Taylor, 9 Ill Inf
Charles Johnson, ship—US Osage (maybe)
Webster Lawrence, 13 Mich Inf
William E. Hester, No Unit Given
John L. York, No Unit given
Richard M. Phillips, 21 Ind Inf
Isaac Golightly, 6 Ill Inf
William Collier, 81 Ill Inf
John Brodhacker, 50 MO Militia
John H. Miller, 10 Tenn Cav
James H. Parker, 131 Ill Cav
Lewis Brodhacker,, 50 MO Cav
Louisa Cooper widow of Samuel H. Cooper, 6 Ill Cav
John W. Prefsow , 7 Tenn Cav
David F. Buckman, 32 Ill Inf
Marcus G. Settles, No Unit Given
Columbus A. Fox, 5 __ Cav

Nathan M. Colley, No Unit Given
Daniel Falkner, No Unit Given
Samuel A. Adams, No Unit Given
William H. Morris, No Unit Given
Henry H. Tray, No Unit Given,
Martha Rogers widow of Charles Rogers, No Unit Given
Jeremiah Gullion, No Unit Given
Elmaee F. Mackin widow of _____, No Unit Given

NEW MADRID CO. MISSOURI

The following abbreviations were used on the census: MO for Missouri, IL for Illinois, IN for Indiana, NJ for New Jersey, NY for New York, Pa or Penn for Pennsylvania, Tenn for Tennessee, KY for Kentucky, Kan for Kansas, Ark for Arkansas, Mich for Michigan, Wis for Wisconsin, CT for Connecticut, NC for North Carolina, Ala for Alabama, Inf for infantry, Cav for cavalry, Lt for light, art for artillery, vol for volunteer, USS for United States Soldier, Col for colored, Reg for regiment, Vet for veteran, res for reserve, and Tel for Telegraph.

NAME—UNIT

Allen, David T., 39 IL Inf
Stepp, James D., 2 MO Inf
Tanner, Andrew J., 39 IL Inf
Lee, James M., 50 MO Inf
Divinney, James R., No Unit Given
Presson, Henry T., 7 TN Cav
Holden, Francis M., 16 KY Cav
Crump, Jacob, 8 MO Cav
Gossett, John, 35 KY Inf
Wilson, Andrew J., 120 IN Inf
Jane Kerr widow of Daniel Kerr, 58 MO Inf
Norwood, Samuel, No Unit Given
Hildreth, William P., 8 KY Cav
William H. Andrews, Sol US
John Ford, Sol US
Elizabeth Johnson widow, US S
Margella Nations widow, US S
Margaret A. Blessing widow, US S
Eloria Ward widow, US S
Delia Brown widow, US S
Noah Woolsey, Confederate, ship Susquehanna
Samuel W. Cobb, 65 IN Inf
William _.__usby, 42 IN Inf
McKinney Marcus, 6 MO Inf
John Mathews, 12 KY
Michel Koch, 23 IN Inf
Ephraim Browiza, 28 IN Cav
Francis M. Sparks, 1 Ala Cav
Charles R. Ball, 49 Ohio Inf
William B. Zimmerman, 19 Penn Inf
Spar_ies Razain, 4 IL Cav
Danial Gorman, 138 IN Inf
Danial Bumap, 21 Ohio Inf
Eilkama Allison, 91 IN Inf
John Harding, 20 IL Inf
Hall, Edward T., o Unit Given
Ruggles, Charles L., No Unit given
Webb, William M., No Unit given
Kitterman, David, No Unit Given
Huntington, Charles, 127 NY Vol.

McKinney, George H., 65 IN Inf
Gileto, William C., 42 IN Inf
Stratten, John, No Unit Given
Farmer, William S., 3 KY Cav (May be Confederate)
Ryall, Hope, widow USA, 15 WVa Inf
Ryall, George W., 1 IN Cav
Brinkley, Frederick, M., 17 KY Cav
Hillix, Geo. W., 16 IL Cav
Gloria widow of James Slinton,, 2 Ark Cav
Davis, Nannie E. widow US Sol, 6 TN Cav
Bishop, Abner, No Unit Given
Earney, John, 21 IL Inf
Martin, Thomas, No Unit Given
Haynes, Edw. Brake, 138 IL Vol
Frazier, Robert, No Unit Given
Wolsey, James H, No Unit Given
McPaff, Mathew, 7 IN Cav
Johnson, James, 1d (Could be IN) Heavy Arty
Miller, Medora Gray widow of Jas. P. Miller, MO Cav
Banks, Mark, 18 US Col.
Mowery, Chas. A. 1 US (New Hampshire) Cav
Barnes, S. S., Cabin Stewart, No Ship Given
Reese, Elmer G., 149 NY
Baker, Peter, 50 MO Inf
Welshans, Robert D., 1 MSN V (I don't know what this is—could be Missouri State Militia Volunteer)
McDonald, Finley, 35 KY Inf
Horibon, Frederic, US Steamer Peoria
Pompey, Hunter, No Unit Given
Wm. Martin, Sol
Annanis Chism, Sol
Frank Reid, Sol
Charles Reed, Sol
Rache E. widow of Hiram Barker, Sol
Wm. Hinny, Sol
Samuel Yates, Sol
Josephine Jones widow of Edward Jones, Sol
Stephen St.Many, Sol
James Grapham, Sol

Wm. L. Coates, Sol
Henry Thomas, Sol
Albert F. Fellows, Sol
Henry Renfroe, Sol
William R. Earley, 26 KY Inf
Thomas R. Pangle, 3 TN Cav
Peter Hochm, 1 MO St Militia
George Dallas, No Unit Given
Fred Palmier, 18 MO Inf
Robert Parker, 14 IL Heavy Art
William Mayberry, 13 Penn Cav
William King, 122 Ohio Inf
Harvey L. Shidler, 115 Ohio Inf
Amos Barnes, 50 MO Inf
Hugh D. Quigley, 29 IL Inf
Howard F. Beymer, 1 MO Cav
George W. Shirkey, 156 IL Inf
John J. Stewart, 31 Wisc. Inf
Anthonny Richardson, No Unit Given
John W. Hunter, 1 Ala Cav
John Pickard, 98 IL Inf
Abram Sarrls, 131 IL Inf
William Ware, No Unit Given
Charles F. Madic, No Unit Given
Daniel Nukolas, No Unit Given
Thomas Rochell, No Unit Given
John Tracy, No Unit Given
Becky Swader widow of Swader, No Unit Given
John Stickney, No Unit Given
Fanny Brown widow of James Brown, No Unit Given
Andrew J. Wheeler, 58 IN Inf
Francis G. Lockett, 35 KY Inf
Thomas J. Blackwell, 55 KY Inf
James Hatcher, 11 IL Cav
Patrick H. Aldridge, 17 KY Cav
Robert Tucker, 3 KY Cav (could be Confederate)
William R. Poe, 22 KY Inf
Caflin, James, 35 IL Inf
Mitchell, Charles, 3 MO Cav
Inzer, William J., 13 IL Cav
Sinks, Charles alias Danial Coryell, 10 IL Cav
James Stublefield, 20 KY Inf
Barliff, Richard, 5 VA Inf
Elizabeth Barnes, widow US Sol.
John J. Henson, US Sol
Isaac Obanon, US Sol
Geo. W. Brewer, US Sol

OREGON CO. MISSOURI

The following standard abbreviations were used: KY and Ken for Kentucky, Inf for Infantry, Cav for Cavalry, MO for Missouri, NY for New York, Tenn for Tennessee, IL for Illinois, IN for Indiana, Lt for light, Art for artillery, Ark for Arkansas, LA for Louisiana, Penn and PA for Pennsylvania, NeH for New Hampshire, Mich for Michigan, Me for Maine, Miss for Mississippi, Wisc for Wisconsin, Sol for soldier, Mtd for Mounted.

This county had a large number of Confederates show up on the census.

NAME/UNIT

William Wilson, 47 KY Inf
Harvey Busby, Confederate, 2 MO Cav
Nallburriss, L. Mathews, Confederate, 2 MO Cav
Ira G. Hall (Hull) Confederate, 2 MO Cav
Benjamin Shahurn, Confederate, 2 MO Inf
Semore T. Williams, Confederate, 2 MO Inf
James W. Bowell, Confederate, 2 MO Inf
Arion, Lewis, Confederate, 2 MO Cav
Christopher Milsap, 3 MO Cav
James McLaughlin, 14 NY Inf
James A. Clark, 2 Tenn Inf
John A. Whiten, Confederate, 2 MO Inf
Sermort, W. Green, Confederate, 2 MO Cav
Lemuel A. Martin, 2 MO Cav
William M. _ogel, Confederate, 8 KY Inf
Danirl Germon, 1 IN
Henry Nesbitt, 69 NY Inf
James Rhietenhoer, Confederate, 10 MO Cav
James Dr___y, Confederate, 2 MO Cav
John W. Watson, 1 MO Inf
Henry Higgins, 40 MO Inf, 70 IN Inf
John Hoftrin, Confederate, 24 Tenn Inf
Aelum, Strawsnieter, 31 IN Inf
John F. Short, Confederate 2 MO Cav
James M. Short, Confederate, 2 MO Cav
Benjamin Gum, Confederate, 2 MO Cav
Samuel Ross, 31 IN Inf
James T. Ab____m, Confederate, 2 MO Cav
McClure, Wm. B., No Unit Given
Jessee W. Walker, 110 IL Inf
Andrew J. Lisby, Confederate, 3 MO Cav
Jesse Nasalood, KY Lt. Art
James B. Old, Confederate, 4 MO Inf
Andrew J. Bellok, Confederate, MO Cav
Thomas W_ngles, Confederate, No Unit Given
William D. Ransorce, 17 KY Cav
William A. Reed, No Unit Given
Nancy widow of Jokas Moore, No Unit Given
James W. Eaker, 27 MO Cav
Oliver Linggure, Confederate, No Unit Given
Jessee Lewis, Confederate, No Unit Given
William D. Lam, No Unit Given
Daniel C. Henry, No Unit Given
Sarah Thomas widow, Confederate, No Unit Given
Philip A. Arbrgust, Confederate, MO Cav
Wm. A. Canttrell, No Unit Given
John N. Alkose, No Unit Given
Seth Boles, No Unit Given
George Huddlest__, Confederate, No Unit Given
Martin Griffith, Confederate, No Unit Given
George M. Humphreys, Confederate, No Unit Given
Wm. T. Eakers (Bakers), Confederate, No Unit Given
Tabitha Watson, widow of Bob King, Confederate, No Unit Given
Jones, Sysvester, R. 4 Tenn Art
DePriest, Elizabeth widow, Confederate, No Unit Given
Smith, Jas. H., No Unit Given
Parson, Robert (Robin) E., Confederate, 2 MO Cav
Woodside, James P. Confederate, 4 MO Inf
Woodside, Emily H. widow, No Unit Given
Gra__s, Wm. C., 6 Tenn Cav
Klepter, James M., 4 MO Inf
Lisby, Wm. Confederate, 4 MO Inf
Bartsfield, John, 2 IN Cav
Ragan, John, 4 MO Cav
Huddleston, James, Confederate, 4 MO Inf
Passott, Jese, No Unit Given
Pabmas, Herman, Confederate, 6 TN
Shrum, Elizabeth, widow, Confederate, 4 MO Inf
Possy, J. R., Confederate, TN Cav
Lucia Amelia widow of Campbell, No Unit Given
Judd, Martin M., 1 MO Lt Art

Palmer, D____sa widow, Confederate, No Unit Given
Wilson, Alford, C., 47 KY Inf
Williams, John, Confederate, Ark Inf
Frinds, John, No Unit Given
Law, George W., Confederate, Cav
Park, James A. Confederate, 2 MO Inf
Chastain, Sarah, widow, No Unit Given
Schwappe, John, Confederate, No Unit Given
Parish, _____ru widow, No Unit Given
Gannor, Wm. No Unit
Williard, Wm. 60 IL Inf.
Jolliff, Randol, Confederate, 4 MO Inf
Rambree, Tabitha, former widow of _____, Cav
Royal, Rediana F, Confederate, (60 IL Inf?)
Cor, John, MO Cav
Judd, H., IL Inf
King, Sarah widow of W, King, Confederate, No Unit Given
Willis, Hense, Confederate, No Unit Given
Lewis, Mary formerly widow of Allison, No Unit Given
Lewis, James R., Confederate, MO Inf
Henplsey, Thos. A., No Unit Given
P_g Raskin (Rankin) widow of_____, Confederate, No Unit Given
Giran, William, No Unit Given
D_kan, Calvin R., Confederate, MO Cav
Tom, James H. 60 IL Inf
Williard, James C., 60 IL Inf
Beaty, Sam _., Confederate, 4 MO Cav
Parrish, James S., Confederate, IL Cav
Cryder, Jacob C. W., No Unit Given
Segan, Philip W., No Unit Given
Betts, John, No Unit Given
Holloway, Richard H. 124 IL Inf
Mary widow of Doucet, No Unit Given
Welch, John, No Unit Given
McClellan, Jas. P., 87 IL Cav
Kane, Thomas, No Unit Given
Thorn, William M., 2 LA Inf
Enonwiss (Sp?), Dallas, No Unit Given
Hook, Thomas, No Unit Given
William, Wes M., No Unit Given
Chase, Benjamin F., No Unit Given
Dissney (Denney), Wm. W., No Unit Given
Nee, Cahrian, No Unit Given
Buck, Thomas J., 2 KY Inf
Steed, Isaac F., 40 IL Inf
Key, Elias, No Unit Given
Morse, Walter S., 143 IL Inf
Morton, James T. No Unit Given
Harris, Alf, No Unit Given
Flowers, Wm. F., No Unit given
Allen, Henry, No Unit Given
Forsyth, Elijah, No Unit Given

Wilkenson, Chas. F., No Unit Given
Frith, Stan F., 7 KY Inf
Johnson, Samuel, No Unit Given
Stone, Arch, No Unit Given
McKee, Jno. S., No Unit Given
Titus, Wm.. No Unit Given
Gorris, Dock, No Unit Given
Marris, Jno. S. No Unit Given
Grissom, James, 130 IN Inf
Napp, Huson, No Unit Given
Cooper, Charles, No Unit Given
Arssineta widow of Burrow, Tuedaelt (Sp?), No Unit Given
Frasbie, Philmore, 10 MO Inf
Rich, Lo_____, No Unit Given
Morse, Geo. W., 11 IN Inf
Hutchison, N.S., 194 Ohio Cav
Bracht, Jno. J. No Unit Given
Kirby, Wm. S., 50 MO Inf
Owens, Thomas, No Unit Given
Joule, Frank, 192 Penn Cav
Coussi__, Frank, No Unit Given
Bidegner, Jno. A., No Unit Given
Murrell, Thomas, No Unit Given
Collins, Geo. No Unit Given
Speare, Jake J., 147 IN Cav
Gussiou (Guniou), W. F., 26 IL Inf
Gullie, Chas., 87 IL Inf
Haislett, Otho J., 59 IL Cav
Tiles, Wm. G., No Unit Given
Hampton, Wm., No Unit Given
Hitt, Samuel F., 2 IN Inf
____ten, Joel A., Confederate (this entry badly lined through), 1 Ark Inf
Vaughn, Wm. R., No Unit Given
Ladd, Geo. P., 11 NY Inf
Sims, Harley, 2 NeH (New Hampshire) Cav
Alleci, Henry J., 14 MO Inf
Dennios_, James, 47 IN Inf
Martin, Gilbert _., 57 Ohio Inf
Bedegris, Johnathan H. (lined out) (7 Ohio Cav) no explanation
Meirrell, Thomas (Confederate),(2 US Inf?)
Lincoln, Geo. L. Confederate, No Unit Given
Renefrow, alias Cash, Wm. NO Unit Given
Vincent, Geo M., 13 Ohio Cav
Barrett, Leonard C., 11 IL Inf
Feruslin, Abraham, No Unit Given
Johnson, Thomas, 56 IL Inf
Reed, Geo. W., 193 Ohio Inf
Tiles, F. M., 4 IL Inf
McDonald, Jno. L., 24 MO Inf,
Wheat, Richard R. No Unit Given
Jones, John R., 98 IL Inf
Wilson Newton, 87 IL Inf
Isaac N. Nangester, Soldier

T. J. Batman, Soldier
Riggie Jones, widow
S.L. Martin, Soldier
John W. Ragan, Soldier
James Posnery, Soldier
B.W. Scott, Soldier
Andy Johnson, Soldier
Emily Dorrey (Doney), soldier
Richard Fletcher, soldier
G_____ Olmstead, sailor
Gilbert M. Blankenship, Confederate, No Unit Given
John B. Harper, Confederate, No Unit Given
Japer Resenhoover, Confederate, 1 MO Inf
George B. Norman, Confederate, 47 MO Inf
James A. Foust, Confederate, No Unit Given
Charles A. Booker (Confederate) 1 MO Inf
Daniel McCarty, 3 Ken Cav
(not legible) H. Stone, 14 MO Cav
James Wheeler, No Unit Given
John N. Hays, 73 MO Inf
Nathaniel Callahan, Soldier
Robert N. Bartow (Barton), soldier
Joseph G. Pitchford, 16 MO Cav
William R. Obar, No Unit Given
Henderson M. Chitty, 24 MO Inf
John R. C. Heeber, 80 IL Inf
Albert Dunsmore, 10 Mich Cav
_____Meeks, No Unit Given
Mary Meeks widow of Andrew J. Nipps, 32 Me (MO) Inf
Amos Ballah, 35 IL Inf
Francis N. Gauldnig, 47 MO Inf
William H. Doner, IL Cav
Thomas M. Norman, 3 MO Cav
John N. (U) Norman, 3 MO Cav
James Robinson, Tenn Cav
Cath Thompson widow of James A. Thompson, Confederate, MO Cav
Lextin, Thadeus G., 2 MO Cav
Thomadin, Wm. A., 7 MO Cav
Holland, T. H., Confederate, MO Cav
Welch, B. T. 25 Ohio Inf
Nicholso, J. (crossed out) A. J., Confederate, 10 MO Inf
Beckeman, Joseph, 10 MO Inf
Jonathan Whitten, Confederate 5 MO Inf
James Lisk, 116 PA Inf
Coiner, J. Y., 8 MO Cav
T.M. Simpson, MO State Guard
Wm. R. Boren, 31 IL Inf
Jas. P. Hackworth, Confederate, MO Cav
Robert Bunn, Confederate, MO Cav
Francis M Nettle, Confederate, MO Inf
Joseph C. Underwood, MO Inf

Wm. Phillips Lang, Mary A. Holt, widow of Joseph Holt, Confederate, MO Inf
John Linton, Confederate, Ark. Inf
W. W. Wagner, Confederae, 21 Ark Inf
Henry V. McArthur, 2 Tenn Inf
W. B. Fagan, Ala Cav
Jno. S. Prince, Confederate, 46 Tenn Inf
Angeline Rodman widow of John Rodman, 73 IL Inf
James Pender, 62 IL Inf
Enoch Gaither, 120 IL Inf
Wm. A. Thomasson, Confederate 10 Miss Cav
Alfred H. Irby, Confederate, 7 Ark Cav
Wm. S. Buckner, Confederate, MO Inf
Andrew J. Curtis, 8 Wisc. Inf
Frederick Newton, 17 Wisc Inf
Charles Millen, 128 IL Inf
Retin S. Simpson, Confederate 1 MO Inf
M. M. Dobbs, Confederate, MO Cav
Wm. W. Lynn, Sol
Wm. W. Trask, Sol
James Barton, 2 MO Lt. Art
Nancy widow of Elisha McGehee, 6 MO Cav
James K. P. Conner, 92 IN Inf
William A. Preston, 15 MO Cav
Nancy widow of William M. Ginnis (McGinnis), No Unit Given
Isaac S. Anderson, 4 Ark Mtd. Inf
James B. Bryant, No Unit Given
Susan E. McDonald, widow, NoUnit Given
Brewer, Josiah, 2 Tenn Mtd. Inf
Joseph Fletcher alias John W. Henley, 1 MO Cav
Shipton, William _., 2 Ark Cav
Thompson, John F., 8 KY Cav
Baughman, Jacob H., 34 IL Inf
Johnson, Benjamin _., 50 MO Inf
Tegrie, James R., 35 KY Inf
Roy Nix, No Unit Given
Roberts, William, 51 IN Inf
Kimes Benton, 7 Ohio Art
Smith, William A., 14 MO Cav
Harris, James W., 91 IL
Burns, Ra___ T., 14 KY Vol.
Bridges, William I., 113 IL Inf
Mallory, James R., 5 NY Cav
Johnson, Danil R., 50 MO Inf
Black, Thomas W., 49 IN inf
Brelsford, Daniel H. 133 Ohio Inf
Holliday, William H. 119 IL Inf
Burns, Joseph _., 145 IL Inf
Chafins, John W., 91 IL Inf
Lefever, William A. 64 Ohio Inf
Jacob C. Smith, 64 Ohio Inf
Jerry Black, 49 IN Inf
Artha (Ortha) G. Remmick, soldier US
William G. Cantrell, Soldier US

Cousins, David E., 70 IL Inf
Hoover, Jonas S., 62 IL Inf
Anderson, William G., 14 Iowa Inf
Missouri Jones widow of William _. Jones, 118 IL Inf
Malinda M. widow of James M. Test, 13 MO Cav
Nancy, widow of William J. Neale, 5 Tenn
Rebecca N. widow of James Vanwinkle, 159 Ohio Inf
Verbrych, William, 5 Ohio Cav

PEMISCOT CO. MISSOURI

The following standard abbreviations are used: Sold for soldier, wid for widow, IN for Indiana, Inf for infantry, IL for Illinois, Wis for Wisconsin, Cav for cavalry, Tenn for Tennessee, MO for Missouri, NY for New York, KY for Kentucky, Minn for Minnesota, art for artillery, v or vol for volunteer, r for reserve, mtd for mounted, lt. for light.

NAME/UNIT

William H. Martin, Sold
Phillip M. Whitten, Sold
Joseph W. Layton, Sold
William Bradshaw, Sold
John H. Landers, Soldier
William R. Hersell, Soldier
Alexander Vaughn, Soldier
Emma A. Parmer (wid), Soldier
John T. Ro_c, Soldier
D. C. Coburn, Soldier
Joseph O. Davis, 128 IN Inf
Soloman J. Owens, 134 IL Inf
William R. Hartwell, 82 IN Inf
Richard T. Dudley, 36 Ohio Inf
John Colinraw, 209 IL Inf
Roy Gaskins, 18 IL Inf
Henry B. Reeves, 122 IL Inf
John C. Furman, 2 Wis. Cav
Philip P. Crooks, 135 IN Inf
George Prellurn, 4 Tenn Cav
Charity P. Caplis widow of Reuben Caplis, 50 MO Inf
Talbert Riddle, 4 Tenn Inf
Thos. J. Evans, 8 Tenn Inf
John R. Grover, 61 IL Inf
Louisa Sprinkles widow of William T. Sprinkles, 44 IN Inf
John W. Jones, 22 IL Inf
Daniel Stokley, 58 IN Inf
Green B. Lynch, 81 KY Inf
Ben F. Allen, 173 Ohio Inf
Robert Belson, 2 IL Cav
H. C. Tharp, 1 Minn Art
Cornelius O. Orgon, 15 IL Inf
G. W. McConnell, 2 MO Cav
D. Z. Alexander, 6 Tenn Cav
Sharp, Robert M., 26 IN Inf
Alvey, William T., 13 IN Cav
Rebecca A. widow of Brush, Jonathan, 15 V R Corps

Adams, Z. U., 13 IL Cav
Adams, Rilry, 29 IL Inf
D_____, widow of Humphrey, Forney H., 12 IL Inf
Burns, James P., 63 IN Inf
N___son, William F.-Hattie A. widow of, 62 MOInf
Hillard,_____, No Unit Given
Graham, Martin V., 10 Tenn Inf
Johnson, Jacob, 4 US Heavy Art
Fristodh (Fristodn), Charles, sailor, ship— Conestoga
Drewprey, Abraham, 1 MO Inf
Read, James B., 6 Tenn Cav
Lambbin, David N., 60 IN Inf
Noble, Felix F., 17 IN Inf
Ea__tt,__org_ (illegible), 50 MO Inf
Abboth (Abbott), Jonathan, 6 IL Cav
_erederson, _____ H., 26 Ohio Inf
Hurst, August, 6 IN Inf
James Uisrol_a, 66 IN Inf
Parthenia widow of John W. Carr, 2 Tenn Inf
Ralls, Lemuel, 4 US Heavy Art
Elder (Elden), William, 8 IN Inf
McCrup____, Francis M., Tenn Inf
Fo_____(illegible), 81 IN Inf
Washington, George, 65 MO Inf
Elizabeth widow of John Manning, 2nd Texas Vol.
William H. Grayson, 56 IN Inf
John W. Anderson, 45 IL Inf
Thomas T. Thompson, 1 Tenn Inf
Thomas B. Griffin, 7 Tenn Cav
James R. Tittle, 63 Ohio Inf
Charles R. Mitchell, 107 NY Inf
Nelson J. Bull (Beell), 3 KY Cav
John Gardner, 31 IL Inf
William W. Hendrix, 59 IL Inf
Jake (John) W. Lane, 40 IL Inf
Luke Cassidy, 35 IN Inf
George W. Little, 35 IN Inf
Anthony Sheily, (Sherley), 10 KY Inf

Henry Flowers, 7 Tenn Cav
Patrick Fowler, 53 IN Inf
Isaac McKay, US Sold
Henry Burton, US Sold
Sarah E. Sikes (US widow), widow, US Sold
George W. Wood, US Sold
Richard M. Thomas, 35 KY Mtd Inf
Simpson G. Hampton, 1 KY Lt. Art, 120 (20) IL Inf
J. Henry Field, Sol
Thomas C. Chuk, 49 IL Inf
James L. Lester, 50 MO Inf
Enoch R. Pullam, Sol, No Unit Given
Cyntha J. Tucker, widow Sold.

PERRY COUNTY MISSOURI

The following abbreviations were used on the census: Inf for infantry, cav for cavalry, art or arty for artillery, Ind for Indiana, Ill for Illinois, Ala for Alabama, Wisc for Wisconsin, NY for New York, VA for Virginia, PA for Pennsylvania, MO for Missouri, Oh for Ohio, S for soldier, col for colored, Battn for battalion, Sol for soldier.

Name/Unit

James B. Hudson, 36 MO Inf
Edward Pellirn, 38 MO Inf
_____ U.E. Canter, Ohio Inf
David Duckworth, 50 Ind. Inf
John Hardinger, 4 (could be 1) MO Inf
Thomas J. Skaggs, 50 MO Inf
Sarah Williams widow of Francis Williams, 50 MO Inf
John H. Knollhoff, Sol
James Powers, Sol
William Edmond, 51 MO Inf
Jefferson Yount, 47 MO Inf
Henry Yount, 12 MO Cav
Mary E. Carricks widow of William D. Cru___, 50 MO Inf
William Lee, 50 MO Inf
Z_blert Bess, 47 MO Inf
Obrebery Buckey, 47 MO Inf
William P. Freeman, 30 MO Cav
James P. Lee, 3 MO Cav
Andrew E. G. Pevine, 1 Wisc. Cav
Carl Thompson, 47 MO Inf
Lawson Thompson, 50 MO Inf
Jah C. Thompson, 50 MO Inf
Theodore Geile, 2 MO Inf
John Babwin, 128 Ill Inf
Amandy widow of August Heitman, 50 MO Inf
Andrew J. Labur, 109 NY Inf
John Mullins, 50 MO Inf
William Engas, 50 MO Inf
Frederick E. Kaltkamer, 11 MO Inf
Peter Miller, 13 Ind. Inf
Ablearand French, 47 MO Inf
Alexander Tornbaugh, 14 MO Cav
Mary A. widow of Vallian Parres, 47 MO Inf
Joseph B. Tricher, 47 MO Inf
Thomas Durvall, 12 MO Cav
Jaline W. McDowell, MO Cav
Joseph Shremp, 47 MO Inf
Francis Haddock, 47 MO Inf
Godfred Blesseng, 20 MO Inf

Peter Nisler, No Unit Given
George N. Roberson, 47 MO Inf
Lewis Black, No Unit Given
Joseph Chandler, 50 MO Inf
Peter Millfalill, MO Cav
Martin Doll, MO Cav
Ferrole Credin, 80 Ill Inf
Thomas Hearn, 47 MO Inf
William G. Hearn, 5 MO Inf
Charles Ticher, 50 MO Inf
William R. Cecil, 47 MO Inf
Benjamin Mowser, 47 MO Inf
Joel Cash, 11 Ind. Inf
Jame Danely, 68 MO Cav
Catherine former widow of Green, Baler, No Unit Given
James Ken-ard, 21 MO Inf
Mary L. Martin widow of Jeptha Martin, 5 MO Cav
Johnathan Dennis, 50 MO Inf
Francis M. Young, 47 MO Inf
Johanna C. A. widow of Frederich Nennest, 29 MO Inf
Martin Crosby, 152 Ill Inf
Joseph Goetz, No Unit Given
Lonead J. Leibel, No Unit Given
Litchen Holschen, No Unit Given
F. D. Holschen, No Unit Given
Parel Lembach, No Unit Given
Wm. H. Goehe (Goeke), No Unit Given
Frederich Nennest, No Unit Given
Michael Fasaold J., 5 MO Cav
Josephine widow of Dubois, Joseph, 5 MO State Militia
Napoleon Certhemy, 30 MO Inf
Joseph F. Shelby, 47 MO Inf
Elizabeth widow of Joseph Nunster, 47 MO Inf
Andrew Bolsman, 2 MO Art
John D. Stempe, 154 Ill Inf
Frances Lukfahr, 47 MO Inf
Christian Kofer, 3 MO Inf
Jesse Myers, 47 MO Inf
George P. Blaylock, 47 MO Inf
Charles Lobarger, 50 MO Inf
Albert T. Crow, 50 MO Inf
John S. Blaylock, 47 MO Inf
Ephraim, Backs, 5 MO State Militia Cav

Thomas Stone, 47 MO Inf
Joseph T. Weiss, 2 MO Inf
John B. Zohner, No Unit Given
Charles F. Besand, Sol. No Unit Given
Louis Fogel, Sol. No Unit Given
Henry Herin, 2 MO Art
John Meyer, 43 Ill
Fritz Goeler (Gorlen), 23 MO Inf
Smannel, Lubel, U.S. Sol
George Koffman, Soldier
Calvin Fisher, U.S. Sol
Anna M. Oberndorfer, widow, U.S. Sol
Threasa Wagner, widow U.S. Sol
John Meyer, U.S. Sol
Charles W. Baelense, Soldier
Louisa Schroter, widow, U.S. Sol
Gattfriett Wachter, U.S. Sol
John Hilpert, Soldier
John Millitzer, Soldier
Wingerter, Joseph, 154 Ill Inf
Hpinkle, John F., 5 MO Cav
Franklin, Giebhard, 4 MO
Frank Winkler, 50 MO Inf
Maria W. formerly widow of Joseph Schott, 8 MO Inf
Alfred Gillerwater, 125 NY Cav
William Wacher, 50 MO Inf
Joseph H. Untereener, 50 MO Inf
John T. Boon, 20 Ill Inf
Henry Hennemaner, 2 MO Art
Herman Funke, 4 MO Cav
John Winkler, 8 MO Inf
Emmanuel Urban, 8 MO Inf
John E. Gorden, 50 MO Inf
John Schnerner, No Unit Given
Gabriel Bronenkant, 26 MO Inf
Stephen Winkler, 50 MO Inf
Elias Garris (Gorris), 13 Ill Cav
Alexander Hull, Sol. US exempted
Jasper J. Erwin, 30 MO Inf
John W. Thomas, 142 Ill Inf
Josiah Tucker, 2 MO Arty
_oras B. Resley, 48 Ill
Ellen Baundendistel widow of Nicholas Baundendistel, 30 MO Inf
David R. Inery, 87 PA Inf
Charles R. Dame, 10 Ill Inf
Russel Malleens, 48 MO Inf
John Gray, Confederate, Cav
Michael Canter, 91 Ohio Inf
John Kirnren, 47 Ohio Inf
Mary Leatch widow of Mathew Leatch, 50 MO Inf
Edward Pellerin, 30 Battn MO
Paul Pellerin, 5 MO Cav
Adolpheus A. Allen, 54 Ill Inf

Thomas Vessells, No Unit Given
James B. Hutson, 30 Reg. MO
John Undenger, U.S. Sol
Martha G. widow of Joseph B. Simpson, Confederate
Emile P. (T.) Collir(n), 1 MO Art
Hyppolite Colier, 1 MO Art
Joseph Streiler, 47 MO Inf
Harley Streiler, 47 MO Inf
John B. Klepe enlisted William A. Walker, 4 MO Inf
Not legible/Not legible
Arther Gremand, Home Guard
Henry Nienhaus, E. Malitia
Leaf Saddler, sworn in but not called out Malitia
John Detrich, 38 Ill
George Swan, No Unit Given
Mike Bresleir, 1 (or 7) MO Inf
William Swan, 42 Ill Inf
Levi A. Yarbrough, 50 MO Inf
Robert Clifton, State Militia
Wm. N. Tucker, MO Malitia
Clement G. Tucker, conscript Gen. Bailard
Cresertell-deserted
Julius Kaimsa (Raimsa) 6 MO Militia
William G. Sandler, MO Militia
Furnderson Hebanif---, No Unit Given
Archabad Davidson, No Unit Given
Jacob Rogers, 59 Ind. Inf
Joseph Farrar, Malitia
_____ widow of William M. Farrar, Malitia
Elihus Thompson, No Unit Given
John Warren, 30 MO
John W. Palson, No Unit Given
Francis H. Delapp, MO Militia
Frank Davis, MO Militia
Widow of John Bergonan, Militia
Martin Enders, US
Francis L. Folson, MO Militia
Barney Cashion, MO Malitia
Norman King, State Malitia
Frederic King, State Malitia
Peter G-----, State Malitia
August Laurenze, State Malitia
Richard Swan, State Malitia
Thomas Newberry, US
James M. Warren, East MO Malitia
____urg Abernathy, Malitia
Francis M. Cashion, E. MO Malitia
Ceral W. Cox, Malitia
James Shoults, No Unit Given
Calvin Sandlin, Malitia
Frederic Mehner (Melmer), No Unit Given
Soflora___ home former widow of Michaud, Constant, 5 MO Cav
Meyer, Andrew, 4 MO Inf

Lindner, John, 4 MO Inf
Klobe, Adam, 26 MO Inf
Lux, John, 4 MO Cav
Beane, -u-ie, 47 MO Inf
Cecilia Melis (Nielis) widow of Joseph A (Melis), 5 MO Cav
King, Albert, 19 Ohio Inf
King, Thomas, 39 MO Inf
Sandlin, William, 4 MO Inf
Francis Dubois, 45 MO Inf
Might, constant F. 47 MO Inf
Kenn-k, Henry, 5 MO Cav
Sumes, Emanuel, 47 MO Inf
Hagan, Dennis, 1 MO Art
Richamlet, Aniuel, 4 MO Inf
Elizabeth Brewes widow of B-r-, William, 4 MO Inf
Laflon, Seman, 50 MO Inf
Luvinia, Eleden, widow of John Elden, 30 MO Inf
Tucker, Henry J. 12 MO Cav
Gorman, Andrew, 5 MO Cav
Tucker, Charles L. 50 MO Inf
Paff, Christopher, 50 MO Inf
Lubra---,Anton, 47 MO Inf
Choppins, Casemire, 4 VA (PA) Inf
Gibbon, Nucholas, 4 VA (PA)Inf
W-r, Charles A., 47 MO Inf
Pannier, Jules J., 5 MO Cav
Mary C. Ornana widow or Ornana, Polrick, 47 MO Inf
Susan C. Wilkinson widow of Wilkerson, William T., 30 MO Inf
Fussold, Henry, 1 MO Inf
Springer, Furitz, 1 MO Inf
Arimda Brewer widow of Brewer, Willie L., 1 MO Cav
Mary L. Lufton widow of Lufton, Lewis, 47 MO Inf
Hayden, William A., 80 Ill Inf
Sleiber, Frank, 2 MO Art
Tucker, Simon S., 4 MO Inf
Gibbon, An-t-r, 2 MO Cav
Zolner, Paul _., 4 MO Cav
McBridge, William D., 10 KY Inf
Collier, Anson, 5 MO Cav
Mockmont, Henry, 5 MO Cav
Cina W. A Belrus widow of Bilnus, Henry, 8 MO Inf
Johana Lurye former widow of Charles Krolhapp, 1 MO Art
Possenbach, Louis, 8 MO Inf
Durwin, John, 1 MO Cav
Barbarie Huber widow of Huber, Joseph F., 8 KY Cav
Dillinger, James, 7 MO Inf

_____, Thomas, 4 MO Inf
Cuddenbach, Joseph, 1 Kan Cav
Hoffman, Bernard, 5 MO Cav
Nooss, John, 47 MO Inf
Hunt, Cornelius, 83 Ind. Inf
Josephine French widow of Thomas A. French, 12 MO Cav
Williams, James W., 195 Ohio Inf
Garrah, Christian, 15 MO Inf
Herzog, Lawrence, 33 MO Inf
Hoehn, Gray, 5 MO Cav
McBride, John C., 4 MO Inf
Mary L. Mercier former widow of Alxend Staffings Co. B 30 MO Inf
Augustin Mercier, 5 MO Cav
__rease Montevan widow of Joseph Montevan, 5 MO Cav
Red, John, 97 Ill Inf
Cashfon, Arch N., 5 MO Cav
Lurlin (Turlin), Constant, 30 MO Inf
Kopp, George, 7 MO Inf
Elder, Joseph A., 49 Ill Inf
Turlin, Frank, 5 MO Cav
Mary J. Hoffman widow of Hoffman Leonard J., 47 MO Inf
Lewis, Phillips, 30 MO Inf
John B-zahres, 47 MO Inf
John Beleashear, 47 MO Inf
Fannie Bensoncon, widow of Horrie Bensancon, 5 MO Cav
Valentine, Kempf, 1 MO Cav
Christiane Ridewalt widow US Sol
Elizabeth Hornberger, widow US Sol
Elizabeth Goff, widow US Sol
Bazil Cainbron, 5 MO Cav
Robert B. Holmes, Confederate, No Unit Given
Clotild widow of Micheal McCabe, No Unit Given
James P. Kline, US S
Fred Estes, US S
Wilson Steel, US S
Robert E. McNeely, US S
Lewis Prue, US S
Augustine A Loystow (Loyston), US S
Leo Hagan, US S
James W. Hart, US S
Lewis Cessel, US S
Joseph Moore, US S
Elizabeth Groff, US S
James Karr (Harr), US S
George Ratcliff, US S
Francis M. Hogart, US S
Isaac Smith, US S
William Brown, US S
Jane E. Weiss, US widow
Frank K. Tucker, US S

John Watkins, US S
Austin, Mattingly, US S
August Weiss, US S
Charles C. Frary, US S
Brown, Robert A., 78 MO Inf
Wm. Cairbron, 6 MO
Leonard Thornerire, No Unit Given
Emannuel Smith, No Unit Given
John Grass, 42 Ill
Constant Mourer, No Unit Given
Levi c. Russells, No Unit Given
John H. Hiatt, No Unit Given
James T. Christian, 18 Iowa Inf, 46 Iowa Inf
Welburn W. Roberts, 48 Ill Inf
Hugh Anderson, 22 MO Cav
John Zolener, 1 (could be 7) MO Inf
Tony Shinleinger, 58 Ill Inf
John Bach, 1 MO Inf
Janus Janson (col), 2 MO Inf
Isidore Cessel, 8 MO Cav
Aledander Vessels, 64 MO Inf
Joseph S. Duvall, 13 MO Cav
Eurene Valroy, 30 MO Inf
Balinda J. widow of John Seifurd, 47 MO Inf
Henry Gibear, 42 _____
Henry T. Trueker, 8 MO
Clement J. Fenwick, No Unit Given
Alen Layton, No Unit Given
Thos. V. Layton, 8 MO Cav
Francis X. Miles, No Unit given
Robert M. Brewer, MO State Militia
Trese Cairbron (Gambron) widow of Fairces, Gambron, 5 MO Cav
Robert M. Brewer, 64 MO Inf
Frank S. Smith, No Unit Given
Ellen F. widow of James A. Hash, No Unit given
Sarah widow of Bennie B. Dean, No Unit Given
Romanns Brewer, 64 MO Inf
Thos. W. Robinson, 5 MO Cav
Timothy Brewer, 4 MO Inf
John W. Taylor, 5 MO Cav
Louetta A. widow of John W. Brewer, 47 MO Inf
Samuel Rankins, No Unit Given
Robert Madenson (?), 8 MO inf
Henry Voelker, 4 MO Inf
Clinton Erwin, 5 _____
Isaiah McClure, 13 Oh VA Vol
Chas. McClure, 9 _____
Sarah widow of John A. Krider, 50 Ill
Moses Riney (col), 68 MO Cal
John H. Brown, 3 MO
Benjamin Difani, 78 MO
Geo. H. Cambron, 12 MO
Patrick Williams, 12 MO Cav
John Hof, 22 Ill Inf, 131 Ill Inf, 29 Ill Inf

Charles Hettler, 5 MO Cav
John Dippold, 4 MO Militia
Joseph Amberger, No Unit Given
Lawrence Brown, MO Militia
John F. Dippold, MO Militia
George Winfield, 50 MO Inf
William Brown, MO Militia
Anton Huber, MO Militia
Louise widow of John Zellen, No Unit Given
George Macklin, 10 Ill Inf
Priest Anderson, MO Militia
Louisa widow of Harlin L. Mays, 29 MO Inf
Emily widow of John Endres, 2 MO Militia
Anton Feltz, 5 MO Inf
Arthur B. Parks, 22 Ill Inf
Samuel M. Phillips, 50 MO Inf
Michael Farley, MO State Militia Cav
Vearies Tucker, 47 MO Inf
Moses E. Rule, 59 Ill Inf
Richard Burns, 4 MO Inf
Henry Versehelden, No Unit Given
Hiram L. Buttles, 25 Iowa Inf
Mary Biegler widow of Joseph Biegler, 2 MO Inf
James G. Hagan, 5 MO Cav
Thomas N. Hagan, 47 MO Inf
James Tucker, 142 Ill Inf
Elizabeth Mitchel widow of Samuel Mitchel, 1 Ala Cav
Thomas McClean, 81 Ill Inf
Charles P. Cargile, Confederate, 8 MO Cav
Willie Rector, 47 MO Inf
George Thompson, Wisc. Inf
Jefferson Milliner, 1 Ala Cav
Frederick Layton, 50 MO Inf
Nathan Golden, 30 Ill Inf
Sarah widow of Daniel Esrey, MO Cav
Narcisse Petot, 12 MO Cav
Elizabeth Nations widow of Wiley Nations, Confederate, No Unit Given
Emily Tucker widow of Martin Tucker, No Unit Given
Samuel Favell, Confederate, 7 MO Cav
Pleasant Davenport, Confederate, MO Cav
William Borgerding, 82 Ill Inf
James V. Brewer, MO State Militia Cav
Milton Magar, MO State Militia Inf
Rufus P. Sanders, 50 MO Inf
Miles A. Welty (Weltz), 56 MO Cav
Edward B. Canada, 31 Ill Inf
John Wm, No Unit Given
John C. Ochs, 4 MO State Militia Inf
George firchs, 31 Ind Inf
Isaac G. Chiles, Confederate, 2 MO Cav
James R. Hogan, 47 MO Cav
James H. Butler, 16 Ill Inf

Henderson Holybee, Sol US
Lydia J. Arnold widow of US Soldier
Alexander Grass, Soldier

REYNOLDS COUNTY MISSOURI

The Following abbreviations were used: MO for Missouri, Ill for Illinois, Ind for Indiana, Kan for Kansas, Tenn for Tennessee, Ken or KY for Kentucky, Cav for Cavalry, Inf for infantry, Sol for soldier, NY for New York, Wisc for Wisconsin, Art for artillery, Ark for Arkansas, Bat for battery or battalion.

NAME/UNIT

Francis M. Parker, 97 Ill Inf
Joseph Thompson, 29 MO Inf
Michael Mueller, 43 Ill Inf
Thomas Eliott, 14 MO Cav
William H. Bonney, 2 MO Art
James G. Roe, 3 MO Cav
Henry C. Bonney, 3 MO Cav
Martha widow of Peter Sutton, 47 MO Cav
James H. Evans, 173 Ohio Inf
Dondel C. Bonney, 3 MO Cav
Lewis H. Delashnitt, Sol U.S.
Letha M. Scott, widow, Sol U.S.
James H. Parker, Confederate, No Unit Given
William Shy, Confederate, No Unit Given
Andrew McCoy, Sol U.S.
John D. Snodgrass, Sol U.S.
Charles H. Hodges, Sol U.S.
William D. Strickland, 31 MO Inf
Joseph Kirkpatric, 5 MO Inf
Samuel _. Yates, 173 Ohio Inf
Jacob Shrum, 31 Ill Inf
Jackson Cauley, 91 Ohio
James J. Fortner, 60 MO Inf
Cornelius Sutton, 47 MO Inf
Benjamin F. Cozine on discharge as Franklin Cozun, 14 MO Cav
Edward Leavey, 5 Ind Cav
Sarah A. Johnson widow of Colinan Miner, 3 MO State Militia Cav
James Radford, 3 MO State Militia Cav
Azariah R. Anderson, 12 MO Cav
William S. Troutman, 3 Tenn Inf
John A. Martin, 3 MO Cav
Charles N. Bardsley, 5 MO Cav
Gilead F. Ball, 3 MO Cav
William H. Davis, Freemonts Body Guard
John A. W. Russell, 6 MO Cav
Sargent Wisdom, 32 MO Inf
Moses H. Bell, Merrells Horse
Isaac D. Brown, East MO Militia
James M. Johnston, 47 MO Inf
Wesley W. Carver, 13 MO Inf
William M. Johnston, 10 MO Cav
Cassandra Withrow widow of George Withrow, 32 East MO Militia
Benjamin Roderick, 10 MO Cav
Daniel J. Smith, 32 East MO Militia
Morris M. Adams, 3 MO State Militia Cav
Benjamin N. Gaul, 4 MO Cav
James Johnson, 67 NY Inf
William H. Bailey, 47 MO Inf
Henry McLarney, 68 East MO Militia
John Calahan, 14 Ill Cav
James N. Thomas, 29 MO Inf
Laura T. Fillmore widow of Isaac Fillmore, 7 Ill Cav
John Amsden, 3 MO State Militia Cav
Aaron P. Shriver, Sol U.S.
John S. Dobbs, Sol U.S.
Beck, Joseph S., 3 MO Cav
Wadkins, Martin V., East MO Militia
Sutterford, Edward F., 1 MO Light Art
Rebeckey Widger widow of James W. Widger, 47 Ill Inf
Stall, Christian, 173 Ohio Inf
Keever, William P., 50 MO Inf
Parmer, Allen, 2 Kan Cav
Sutterfred, Allen, Confederate, 1 MO Cav
Tripp, Willey, Confederate, 2 MO Inf
Willis, James C., 28 Ill Inf
Patterson, John, Confederate, 28 Tenn Cav
Sublevan, Henry R., 28 Ken Inf
Edmans, James, Confederate, 24 MO Cav
Elizabeth Jordan widow of John Jordan, 1 MO Cav
Strauther, Samuel P., Confederate, 23 MO Cav
Shirshsville, William _., 36 Ohio Inf
Sanders, James M., Confederate, 24 MO Cav
Othomis Waterson, 13 Ill Cav
Caurits, Charles, Confederate, 4 MO Cav
Pogue, Willey L., 1 MO Cav
Levinsburg, Robert C., 32 MO
Thompson, Thomas B., 14 MO Cav
Howard, Elias, 47 MO Inf
Willet, Francis M., 6 MO Cav
Mann, Sarah _. Widow of Isaac Mann, 47 MO Inf
Saunders, John D., 148 Ill Inf
Pratt, John B., 47 MO Inf
Freeman, Jasper S., KY Inf
Willett, Francis G., 6 MO Cav
Alison, Jessey, 58 MO Inf
Colman, John W., 3 MO State Militia

Ealijah, B-ster, 68 MO
Willis, Francis M., 11 KY Inf
Francis E. Stout widow of Ephraim C. Stout, 85 Ill Inf
Elizabeth Sweeney widow of William Sweeney, 3 MO State Militia
Sabin, Alonzo D., 4 Wisc.
Clark, Joel R., 26 MO Inf
Moore, James M., 3 MO State Militia
Haywood, Edmond R., 1 Ark Bat.
Barrus, Thomas S., 47 MO, 3 MO State Militia
Copeland, John, 47 MO
Fort, Ewing, 68 East MO Militia
Temple, Justin, 38 Wisc.
Dickson, Hiram R., 27 MO Inf
Reitely, James, 1 KY
Trobbs, Fladden, 62 MO Inf
John W. Harris, Sol U.S.
J. G. Ford, Sol U.S.
A.P. Duce, Sol U.S.
Stevenson, Robert, 3 MO State Militia
George D. Johnson, 47 MO Inf
Rutha Webb widow of Kara Webb, Confederate, No Unit Given
Alvin C. Wright, Confederate, 19 Tenn Inf
Lewis Miller, 13 Ill
Charles Carter, Confederate, No Unit Given
William Sweasy, 47 MO Inf
Adam Dunkin, 47 MO Inf
Jessie E. Cates, 8 Tenn Inf
William T. Hoskins, 50 MO Inf
William Chilton, 3 MO Cav
James Brown, 32 MO Vol
Elliott Sawyers, 47 MO Inf
William Bane, No Unit Given
Elizabeth Pulliam widow, No Unit Given
George D. Carpenter, 145 Ind Inf
Hale Riles, Confederate, No Unit Given
William A. Farris, Confederate, 4 MO Inf
Wesley A. Middleton, 29 MO Inf
Sampson Sanders, Confederate, 3 MO Inf
Johiphan Jestice, No Unit Given
George W. Brewer, 3 MO Cav
George H. Lee, 49 MO Inf
Jas. H. Skaggs, No Unit Given
Anna Farris widow of L.N. Farris, Confederate, No Unit Given
John Ragfield, Confederate, No Unit Given
Mathias Mauk, 186 Ohio Inf
Jessey L. Baunds, Confederate, No Unit Given

RIPLEY COUNTY MISSOURI

The following abbreviations were used: Tennis and Tenn for Tennessee, Penn for Pennsylvania, Ala for Alabama, NY for New York, Ken and KY for Kentucky, Kan for Kansas, MO for Missouri, ME for Maine Mich for Michigan, Ill for Illinois, Ind for Indiana, Inf for infantry, cav for cavalry, art for artillery, mtd for mounted, Mass for Massachusetts, Eng for Engineer, Battin for Battalion, and colard for colored.

Name/Unit

John Ship, MO Cav
Mike Rawlings, 13 MO Inf
David Haris, 11 Ill Inf
Elex C. Camp, 18 Ind Inf
William Burlson, 3 MO cav
John W. Yates, 3 KY Cav
Henry H. Hill, 1 Ala Cav
Elizabeth Cormbell, No Unit Given
Daniel M. Williams, 49 Ind Inf
Crittendon B. Eaton, 50 MO Inf
John A. Bryant, 17 Ken Inf
Susan J. Brake widow of John M. Hay, 27 Ken
Mary E. Linedley widow of Peter E. Linedley, Pilot-USS Cherokee
James H. McKinney, 48 Ken Inf
Obediah Hudson, MO State Militia
Louis Kernek, 1 NY Eng
Reuben Upshaw, 6 MO Inf
John W. Lomax, 2 Tenn Inf
Frederick Rayurnkle, 211 Penn Inf
Joseph G. Camp, 47 MO Inf
James M. Lacondew, 6 Tenn Cav
Wayne M. Quinn, Lost Discharge-Col Breal Commanded Regiment
Joseph G. Miller, 24 KY Inf
George W. Johnson, came down with measels and discharged
George W. Helton,, came down with measels and discharged
Luneford L. Pinnell, 48 MO Inf
Samuel L. Hatfield, 1 KY Mtd. Inf
Nancy Lunsford widow of Frank P. Lunsford, 3 MO Cav
Joseph L. Keil, 3 MO Cav
Thomas A. Kennon, No Unit Given
Elizabeth Patterson widow of James B. Crowell, served on a gunboat
Hard_ Little, Colonel Emerson's Regiment
William Keel, 38 Ill Inf
William M. Glore, 15 MO Inf
William T. Driver, 5 KY Cav
Thomas E. Chapman, 2 Ark Cav
Martin L. Coonce, 31 Ill Inf
Alexander Barnes, 6 Tenn Colored
Wiley B. Hudson, 8 Tenn Inf
John B. Smithson, 1 MO Cav

John M. Halland, 9 KY Inf
Hutson A. _aith, 87 Ill Inf
Francis J. Lacy, 6 ME (could be MO) Inf
Samuel _. Steel, 31 Ill Inf
Wiley S. Holland, 5 KY Cav
Isaace Bane, 50 MO Inf
Hazen Wardlow, 26 Ind Inf
Henry C. Smith, 4 KY Cav
Hiram Lunsford, 32 MO Inf
Smuel Chestnut, 39 Ohio Inf
Henry A. Schmetzer, 49 Ill Inf
James B. Keel, 47 MO Inf
David C. Dickson, 9 KY Inf
(NEXT THREE VERY VERY FAINT)
    L------H. F------, 13 Ill Inf
    Benjamin F------, 13 Ill Inf
    John M. Ladd, 6 TN Cav

Samuel Harmon, 82 Ind Vol
Andrew J. Davis, 6 Ind Vol
Samuel P. Campbell, Confederate, 6 Tenn Cav
Henry D. Seawel, 16 Tenn Inf
Ezekiel D. Smith, 1 Tenn Mtd Inf
Jams Dobson, 26 Ind Inf
Washington J. Redus, 1 Ala Cav
Jackson Harris, 40 Ill Inf
Alfred S. Cothorn, 2 Tenn Mtd Inf
Luroy Upshaw, Confederate, Ark Inf
John W. Littleton, Confederate, 8 Tenn Cav
Jasper M. Smelser, MO Cav
David R. Redus, 1 Ala Cav
Harriet Grace widow of James L. Grace, 17 KY Vol
Philip W. Ceannis, 1 KY Cav
Joseph M. Panels, MO Cav
Jab H. Robertson, Confederate, 10 tenn Inf
Robert S. McCelenlack, Confederate, 52 Tenn Inf
John M. Joyner, 64 Virginia Mtd. Inf
John W. Ceals, 18 Ill Inf
Nineosh Jackson, 86 Ind Inf
John W. Cohaphian, 71 Ill Inf
Joseph Ball, Soldier
Naylor, William A., 10 Ind Battin
Sarah E. Cable widow of Carl V. Randol, No Further Information
Chas. W. Miller, 2 Iowa Inf, USS Carondolett
Boone, William H., 29 MO Inf

Dennis, Enoch, Steamer Melconule
Bendes, David A., 129 Ind Inf
Catlett, John, 27 Ind Inf
Burbridge, Benjamin, 6 KY Cav
Black, Emily F. widow of David Black, 130 Ill Inf
Crawford, John B., No Unit Give
Collins, Squire P., 10 Tenn Inf
Sharp, James F., 120 Ill Inf
Slack, Morris F., 27 Mass Inf
Fisk, Charles W., 4 Mich Cav
Van Pendle, Charles, 1 MA (could be MO) Inf
Williams, _____ Papers lost and no info
Lereaux, Julius A., 31 Ohio Inf, 188 Ohio Inf
Chadd, Joseph, 8 Ind Inf
Paye, Francis J., 52 KY Inf
Halland, Rebeca widow of Hilland, Isiah, 88 Penn Inf
Naukirk, William B., 23 Ind Inf
Brooks, William A., 47 MO Inf
Bound, Sara W. Widow of Jesse Bounds, 47 MO Inf
Gomas (Gornas), Richard, Muster roll in Wash City
Benjamin F. Johnson, 50 MO Inf
Lutecia widow of Edmon J. Casteel, First Tenn Inf
James Hemphres, 117 Ill Inf
Shibal York, 25 Ind Inf
William Alen, 1 Kan Cav
James N. Keas, 13 Tenn Cav
Elizabeth G. Hawkins widow of Joseph Hawkins, 38 Ind Inf
Jessie F. Green, KY Inf
Jefferson G. Page, 8 KY Cav, 17 KY Cav
Wm. B. Mitchener, Tenn Mtd Inf
Ardenia widow of William Parkerson, 10 Tenn Inf
William B. Collins, 10 Tenn Inf
Alanson B. Belcher, 47 Ohio Inf
Jacob Grafner, 45 Ind Cav
Andrew J. Ashcraft, 5 MO Cav
Abram M. Casteel, Cav
Laurence Powers, 47 MO Inf
John Lance, 40 Ill Inf
Mamiel J. McNav (?), 136 Ill Inf
Samuel H. Day, 81 Ill Inf
Mary A. Burgess widow, No Unit Given
John Murphy, (Scout), No Unit Given
James G. Jackson, 25 Ind
Andrew Burke, 114 Tennessee
Jackson P. Sands, 97 Ill
Satrroy J. Middleton widow of William H. Middleton, 77 Colard
Nancy E. Smith widow of James E. Smith, 9 Illinois

William Lawson, Soldier
William H. White, Soldier
Sherman Hilland, Soldier
Johnathan J. Thomas, Soldier
Abner J. Bruce, Soldier
Benj. C. Perdom, Soldier
Frasis M. Patteson, Soldier
Sarah A. Ferguson, widow, soldier
James Whitaker, Soldier
William N. Jackson, Soldier
William H. Carnes, Soldier
Edward P. Charnes, Soldier
Henry L. Porter, Soldier
P--- S. Ketchum, Soldier
James A. -hahan, Soldier
James M. Belcher, Soldier
Daniel B. Yingling, Soldier
John B. Merrell, Soldier
George W. O'Neal, Soldier
John Bond, Soldier
John S. Hinson, 41 Ill
Porter Hingali, 54 _____
George C. Kellogg, 29 Ohio
Mry E. Ingram widow of Joseph Ingram, 1 Tenn
Henry Laru, 195 Penn
David Hurnlinger, 195 Penn
John Hurnlinger, 195 Penn
Clearice White widow of Samuel W. White, 8 Mich
Lucy J. Mc___itt widow of John M. Mc____itt, 56 Ill
Wilson, Salmon, 80 Ind
Mary Kl___ widow of Theodore Kl____, 2 MO Art
Jesse S. Dumans, Virginia
John R. Browning, 7 Tenn
William M. Perry, 56 Ill, 86 Ill
William J. Frutesfore (?), 77 Ind
William M. Tharn, 52 KY
G---M. Wright widow of Kasemeir H. Wright, 32 Ill
Franklin Venable, 145 Ill
Samuel K. Callurm (?), 10 KY
William Hines, 54 Ind, 10 Ind
William C. Jenkins, 120 Ill
Moses B. Rhodes, 76 Ohio
Hu____ H. Vise, 40 Ill
William J. Poe, 11 Iowa
John H. Lambert, 62 Ill
Samuel Deen, 1 Ill Art
Warren Stone, 78 Penn
Martin Standley, 22 Ind
Thomas E. Osborn, 1 MO
Mary Baurdman, widow of George M. Baurdman, 15 Mich
Thomas D. Maxey, 110 Ill

Michael Mai____, 6 (not legible)
C----B_____, 7 IA Cav
Jefferson _____ (Not legible)
William W. Gurley, 10 Tennis
Greenbery Hase, Soldier
Abraham J. Jolien, Soldier
Mikel Mullin, Soldier
James W. Gain (Gam), Soldier
James W. Russell, Soldier
Emily Stillwell, widow

ST. FRANCOIS COUNTY MISSOURI

The following abbreviations were used: Del for Delaware, MO for Missouri, NY for New York, IL for Illinois, Wisc for Wisconsin, KY and Ken for Kentucky, Tenn for Tennessee, PA and Penn for Pennsylvania, VA for Virginia, Mich for Michigan, MSM for Missouri State Militia, Ark for Arkansas, Neb for Nebraska, OH for Ohio, and IN for Indiana. Also lt for light, art for artillery, cav for cavalry, res for reserve, inf for infantry, vol for volunteer, col for colored, mtd for mounted, sol and sold for soldier.

NAME/UNIT

Miller, William F., 47 MO Inf
Fiottanar, _____, 40 NY Inf
Mell, Peter _., 47 MO Inf
Miller, George A., 6 MO Cav
Krollmeyer, William P., 47 MO Inf
Hertz, Peter, 47 MO Inf
Ruckus, Frederick, 47 MO Inf
Burlbaw, Nicholas, 37 IN Inf
Hopkins, Eli D., No Unit Given
Schmidt, Peter, No Unit Given
Doughty, David J., No Unit Given
Wilson, Geo. M., 2 Wisc Inf
Peers, Luther K., No Unit Given
Green, George, No Unit Given
Flora widow of Plesner, Herman, No Unit Given
Elvins, Ralph, 47 MO Inf
Burnett, John M., 47 MO Inf
McCormick, Jas. R., General
Canduff, Lewis J., 47 MO Inf
Jackson, George W., No Unit Given
Meloy, Francis M., No Unit Given
Mary J. widow of Hammos, William, No Unit Given
Williams, Thomas, No Unit Given
Lang, Thomas, 47 MO Inf
Odgers, Williams, No Unit Given
Treaster, Jacob C., 13 IL Cav
Vaugh, James E., No Unit Given
Story, Douglas F., No Unit Given
Frances E. widow of William L. Tolman, Surgeon, 10 MO Cav
Wescoat, John W., 1 Wisc Cav
Howell, James, No Unit Given
Sleeth (Heeth), Hezekiah, No Unit Given
Kellor, Henry, W., IL
Fannie widow of Jones, Jeremiah, No Unit Given
Robinold, John H., No Unit Given
Catherine M. widow of Helber, Christian, 47 MO Inf
Emma widow of Boswell, Robt. F. O., 6 Tenn Cav
Loring, William, 15 MO Inf
Burke, Seward, 149 IL Inf
Lorenze, Philip, 1 MO Light Art
Amanda widow of Duncan, Benjamin R., 3 MO State Militia Cav
Elizabeth Kelly former widow of Williams, _____, No Unit Given
James Hill, No Unit Given
Sarah M. widow of Brann, McArthur, 47 MO Inf
Agnew, Milton M., 143 IL Inf
John E. Koester, 4 MO Cav
Thomas C. Goodfellow, 130 IL Inf
William G. Shumake, 2 MO Cav
Lucien Aubuchin, 15 MO Inf
Francis E. Lahaz, 47 MO Inf
Morgan P. Smith, 10 MO Cav
Nathan Becket, 47 MO Inf
Thomas G. Lester, 58 MO State Militia
John B. Snead, 47 MO Inf
Francis M. Richardson, 49 Wisc Inf
William A. Kennedy, 8 KY Cav
Francis Janis, 15 MO Inf
Joseph Chaboude, 8 Co Sharpshooter
Charles C. Kanarawurf, 47 MO Inf
Silas M. Asbridge, 48 KY Inf
Lewis Aubuchin, 47 MO Inf
William Kennedy, No Unit Given
Sarah D. Strain widow of U.S. Sol, No Unit Given
Johnson, David, 9 IL Inf, 1 US Vet Inf
Asbridge, Alfred A., 17 KY Cav
Harrison, John E., 47 MO inf
Patrick, Alfred, 27 MO Inf
Cornelius, Zacariah, 22 IL Inf
Dixon, Elizabeth widow of James R. Dixon, MO Inf
Ward, Annie formerly widow of Sullivan, Sea—fride, 143 Ohio Inf
Walker, Ransom A., 102 IL Inf
Walker, Margaret formerly widow of Marler, John J., 31 MO Inf
Campbell, Sarah widow of Campbell, Joseph B., 31 MO Inf
Rinevelt, Johnathan R., 8 IN Inf, Boat—Tyler
E-lly, Everitt H., 142 IL Inf
Conover, W. H. C., 22 NY Cav
Rodgers, Catherine widow of William Rodgers, 5 MO Cav

Hoover, Martha formerly widow of Hancock, Wm., 24 MO Inf
Nolan, Mary A. widow of Peter Nolan, 31 MO Inf, 32 MO Inf
Isiac Mouser, 3 MO Cav
Isaiah Baucom, 3 IL Cav
William H. Parkison, 8 Tenn Mtd. Inf
William S. Frvin, 31 MO Inf
John Burdgette, 2 MO State Militia Cav
Anna Jaster widow of August Jaster, No Unit Given
Frank Arsenma_, 1 MO Lt. Art
Philip A. Wigger, 32 MO Inf
Sarah E. Scott formerly widow of Joseph H. Hawkins, 4 MO State Militia Inf
Thomas Day, 13 MO Inf
William A. Cross, 10 IL Inf
Bernard C. Pittman, 154 IL Inf
Avaline Rodifer widow of James C. Rodifer, 31 MO Inf
William Rangey, 31 MO Inf
James Carroll, 31 MO Inf
James M. Craig, No Unit Given
Stephen J. Barker, 29 MO Inf
Robert A. Campbell, 13 PA Cav
Charles East, 31 MO Inf
Alfred Henson, 27 Ohio, 2 Tenn Inf
William Whitte_, 20 NY Inf
Thomas P. Shumake, 10 MO Cav
George F. Wigger, 50 MO Inf
Elizabeth Beal formerly widow of Stephen Spaulding, No Unit Given
David Spaulding, No Unit given
Joab B. Ringer, 4 MO State Militia Inf
Andrew White, 31 MO Inf
Michael Marler, No Unit Given
Edward Koettlin_, 75 MO
Michael Gerurns (?), No Unit Given
Ingaro widow of James Daugherty, No Unit Given
John W. Henson, 5 VA Vol, 1 VA Vol
John F. Bradley, No Unit Given
Oscar Denise, PA Vol
John Thurman, 47 MO Inf
George Hughes, 10 NY Vol
George W. Hugers, No Unit Given
George R. (A) Manning, 56 Col Inf
Joachim Ruslege, 26 PA Vol
Charles B. Parsons, 4 Mich Vol
Milton Gipson, 3 KY
Thomas H. Wulu_, Sol US
Thomas L. Oleary, 1 MO Lt. Art, 10 MO Cav
Jerry C. Oleary, 80 MO Inf
Mary P. widow of Frederick Hays, No Unit Given
Henry C. Reeder, 47 MO Inf

James M. Thompson, 33 Wisc Vol
Mary Mager widow of Davidson Mager, No Unit Given
Columbus C. Chandler, No Unit Given
Thomas J. Rile, 47 MO Inf
Charles B. Thurman, 47 MO Inf
Inessonia E. widow of William B. Reeder, 3 MO State Militia Cav
William D. Herris, 5 US Vol
John Byington, 47 MO Inf
Hezekiah Ballour, 10 MO Cav, 2 MO Cav
___hill, D. Hamtrin widow of Stewart, No Unit Given
Nathan J. Arman, 31 MO Inf
Henry L. Romyey, No Unit Given
George W. Maker, 10 IN Vol
James W. Trecker, 50 MO
Venture Meloy, 33 MO
A____ Murphy, MO Militia
William Rulleur, 47 MO Inf
Robert Stockwell, Sailor # 143
Charles Koester, Sailor-Junetta
Mildred _. Parkerson widow of Henry Parkerson, No Unit Given
William H. Bryan, 30 IL Vol
Andrew J. Dixon, OH Inf
John A. McClenahan, No Unit Given
Sela J. Bowie widow of Isaac Bowie, No Unit Given
John B. Hart, 47 MO Inf
John Merritt, 47 MO Inf
Hariah V. widow of Wm. A. Kendel, 156 Ohio
John (Jake) A. Connery, 15 MO Inf
Jonathan F. Smith, Independent Guards, 1 Ark Cav
Mathew Dunn, MO State Militia
James Halmes, Forgotten
Augustus Lalamonlier, 11 MO Vol Inf
William R. Gibson, 15 MO Inf
Jame Felgnn, 11 MO Res Cav
Henry Co____, No Unit Given
George W. Fastkal, State Militia
Samel Creglin, State Militia
Francis A. widow of Frederick H. Sturgis, 1 MO Lt. Art
John M. Hetherly, 6 MO Inf
Charles Grotjohn, 21 ___ Inf
John A. Wanpler, 47 MO Inf
William H. Dooley, No Unit Given
William Stone, 5 Tenn Cav
Benjamin Herrington, 14 Mtd. Tenn Inf
Joseph William Thompson 11 (NH)
George N. W. Fucker, 117 Wisc Inf
Milton R. Davis, 2 Iowa Battery
Mary J. Johnston widow of William L. Johnson, 47 MO Inf

John F. Maston, 7 New Ha--- Inf
James R_sel_, 5 Col MSM
John M. Chamberlain, 47 MO Inf, 50 MO Inf
Jessie P. Marks, 47 MO Inf
William H. Marks, 47 MO Inf
Gondore, George W., Unknown
Amelia L. widow of Charles Sharpe, 31 MO Inf
Theresa J. widow of Owsley, George L., 31 MO Inf
Osborne, George, Unknown
Carver, George W., 31 MO Inf
Laura _, widow of Wm. H. Childs, 47 MO Inf
Hosentral, Herman, 2 MO Art
Hasentral, Wilhelmina widow of Osterhone, ____, No Unit Given
Matthews, Elizabeth widow of Matthews, _____, No Unit Given
Mary _. Widow of Noramon, Andrew J., 60 IL Inf
Coly___, Chas. U., No Unit Given
Murphy, William M. 47 MO Inf

THE FOLLOWING ARE VERY FAINT ON THE MICROFILM:
Williams, William P., No Unit Given
Naomi C. widow of Rouze Gifford, 52 IN Inf
Smith, John, No Unit Given
Miller, Frank B. NY Inf
Warren, Thomas H., 2 Ark Inf
Beard, Jesse, No Unit Given
Langley, William B., 35 MO
Stertaina, Frederick, No Unit Given
Laterusie, John B., No Unit Given
Hayes, Lucius, Mich
Higgler, James P., 8 Tenn Cav
Montgomery, _____, No Unit Given
_____ widow of St. Charles, Benjamin, 47 MO Inf
Manning, James, 1 MO Art
O'Bryan, William A., Little Rebel and W. H. B.
Ada_h widow of Aylsson, McGeorge H., MSM Cav
Eberhart, Frederick, No Unit Given
Josephine widow of Und_boise, Charles, No Unit Given
McCoy, Wilbur J., Tenn
Rebecca widow of Boatright, Thomas, 2 MO Lt. Art
Beck, William, 41 MO Inf
Shelton, Daniel, 3 MO Cav
Mary widow of Briery   NO Unit Given
Mary widow of Scuddle, 5 NJ
_____, David, No Unit Given
K_____, Joseph, 28 IL

NOT LEGIBLE, 2 MO Inf
Little, James, No Unit Given

Dietz, George, No Unit Given
Gibson, James, No Unit Given
Julius Crader, 2 MO Art
Hasia H. Brown, 47 MO Inf
Frank Bower, No Unit Given
Henry _losterman, No Unit given
Charles Summers, No Unit Given
E___P. Cain, Confederate, No Unit Given
John McCarter, No Unit Given
Patrick Odonnl, New York
Numan, McFeolainck Hostana, Confederate, No Unit Given
Alpheus Beanstein, 96 NY
Frederick Deyherle, 3 NY
Elizabeth Maning widow of John Manning—veteran of Mexican War
Mary Ottman widow of John Ottman, No Unit Given
Henry Kleesman, 1 MO Art
James Langley, No Unit Given
Morris, Gann, 3 MO Inf
Benjamin Weitzel, US Sol
Abraham Sypher, US Sol
Alferd Burch, 1 VA Lt Art
Henry Elsman, No Unit Given
Andrew T. W_la__s, No Unit Given
Abraham Elser, 47 Ohio
Catherine widow of _____Elder, veteran of Mexican War
John Myers, 3 MO 43 IL
John Bass, US Reserve home guard
Isaac M. Johnson, US
Frederich Le____age, No Unit Given
Thomas Oldham, US Sol Black Hawk War
John Wood, 174 OH Inf
Henry J. Baker, 27 IL Inf
Jame N. Wood, 36 OH Inf
Eli Hauk, 36 OH Inf
Edmond W. Reavis, 24 MO Inf
Henry P. Pearsall, 30 OH
Thomas J. Forbis, 27 Pen (Ten) Cav
Moses P. Wadkins, No Unit Given
Susan Eavis widow of US Sold, NO Unit given
Phillip Yeagar, 35 MO Inf
Albert G. Eavis, 47 MO Inf
John C. Burton (Luston), No Unit Given
Parlee Absher widow, No Unit Given
Joseph A. Jones, No Unit Given
Elizabeth Beaver widow of US Sol, US Sold
Geo. W. B. Calloird, US Sold
Larkin N. McFarland, US Sold
Benjamin Prater, US Sold
Joseph Wigger, US Sold

Alexander Kincaide, US Sold
Phillip Rush, US Sold
William B. thurman, 47 MO Inf
Alfred Scaggs, 6 MO Cav
William R. Turpin, 6 MO Cav
John H. Moore, No Unit Given
Austin R. Kirkendall, 13 OH Cav
James M. Moser, 10 Tenn Inf
William Scaggs, 6 MO Cav
Henry E. Baker, No Unit Given
Andrew J. (G) Williams, 33 MO Inf
Minerva _. Brimm, wife, 5 Del Inf
James F. Yates, 6 MO Inf
George Wahlan, 18 US Inf
Louisa widow of Thomas McLarney, No Unit Given
George Nash, 24 MO Inf
Fieldon Mackley, 144 IN Inf
Samuel J. Timmerman, sailor, Monongehala
August Henry, 50 MO Inf
Francis M. Beevis, 30 MO Inf
John H. Cullry, 18 IL Inf
Frederic A. Cline, 47 MO Reserve Corps
Jane B. Patterson widow of Abram Casey, No Unit Given
Ziekman Monrey, 6 MO Inf
Antonia Wyeges, No Unit Given
James R. Reuly, 1 US Vol E
Jesse M. Elvins, No Unit Given
Melvin R. Matthews, No Unit Given
James M. Maness, 5 MO Mtd Inf
Jefferson Milner, 33 MO Inf
Andrew J. Chapman, 63 IL Inf
Edwin C. Bloom, 21 MO Inf
James M. Toombs, 2 Ten Mtd Inf
John W. Smith, NY
Henry W. Meyer, 13 MO Inf
Caroline widow of Alexander Trecker, No Unit Given
William Spaugh, No Unit Given
JamesM. Hulsey, 5 IL Cav
Henry Doer, No Unit Given
Francis M. Miller, No Unit Given
John C. Eddington, No Unit Given
James Colston, No Unit Given
Henry Zimmerman, 2 MO Inf
William M. Tollen, 42 IL Inf
James P. McFarland, 50 MO Inf
Peter West, 174 OH Inf
James H. Belmar, 1 Col Vol
Joseph Zimmer, 6 MO Cav
Henry Brineker, 22 OH Inf
Benjamin D. Warnick, 6 MO Inf
Jacob Mehring, 21 MO Inf
Frederick Elser, 120 OH Inf
John L. Lovoarn, 50 MO Inf

William Lulman, No Unit Given
Charles Wineburner, 5 US Art
Daniel Davidson, 5 Neb Cav
Moses Middleton, 50 MO Inf
Maleda Nennrish widow of Frederick Hern___, 1 MO Lt Art
Larkin A. McFarland, No Unit Given
John M. C__ardgard, 33 MO Inf
Louisa widow of Conrad Nieders, 47 MO Inf
Godfrey Birch, 59 OH Inf
Wm. J. Ritter, 32 Ken Inf
Jackson Shaner, No Unit Given
Wm. W. Shaner, 50 MO Vol
James R. Davis, 21 MO Inf
Susan widow of Radford Davis, No Unit Given
Alexander Williams, 15 IL Cav
Martha E. widow of Chas E. Crane, No Unit Given
Cyrus A. Loore, Marne Badger
Louis M. Hardin, No Unit given
Richard S. Forshe, 50 MO Inf
Chas. Politte, 26 MO Inf
Robert F. Robinson, 50 MO Inf
Alia A. Paris former widow of _____ Paris, No Unit Given
Wm. H. White, 50 MO Inf
Henry Cevrman, 85 IN Inf
Lon (Tom) Meiger, No Unit Given
John R. Kirkpatrick, 2 US Inf
George Banister, No Unit Given
James C. Smith, 33 MO Inf
Simon Baker, 5 Ark Inf
John McCombr, 3 US Cav
Isaac Serguet, 2 MO Cav
Hubert Moyne, 2 MO Cav
Wm. A. Scance, 28 US Inf
C. Scance, 37 MO Cav
Francis M. Forchee, 31 MO Inf
Daniel Taylor, No Unit Given
Samuel Kelley, under Gen. Steele
Minerva Birch former widow of Daniel Taylor, No Unit Given
Sarah Fulton widow of Alexander Fulton, No Unit Given
Franklin D. Heaton, 31 MO Inf
George Baker, 3 Ark Inf
William D. Harris, 10 MO Cav
Jonathan Lewis, No Unit Given
John H. Franklin, 30 MO Inf
Elizabeth Trippe widow of Walter Tryppe, 24 MO Inf
Sarah Cookscy widow of David Cookscy, No Unit Given
James Murphy, 6 MO Cav
John Ferguson, 3 MO Cav

Levina Blackwell former widow of Harvey Pinson, No Unit given
Lewis L. Buyer, 50 MO Inf
George Marler, Inf
Nathan L. Day, 103 IL Inf
Monroe Shannon, No Unit Given
Susan Glore widow of US Sold, No Unit Given
John F. Cowan, Sol US
William Pratt, Sol US
John Dosing, Sol US

ST. GENEVIEVE COUNTY MISSOURI

The following abbreviations were used: Inf for infantry, Cav for cavalry, Lt. Art for Light Artillery, Art for Artillery, Col'd for colored, Mtd for mounted, Gov for government, Vol for volunteer, sol for soldier, wid for widow, MO for Missouri, Ill and IL for Illinois, IN for Indiana, Kan for Kansas, NJ for New Jersey, NY for New York, NH for New Hampshire, VA for Virginia, Ark for Arkansas, IA for Iowa and GA for Georgia

NAME/UNIT
Eckert, Anton, 78 MO Inf
Gisi, Augustus, No Unit Given
Grieshaber, Kilian, 78 MO Cav
Lafleur, Mikel, No Unit Given
Olive widow of Brown, Rubin G., 2 MO Cav
Burle, Louis, 41 MO Inf, LA Inf
Bontz, _____, 47 MO Inf
Hoock, Aranie, S., 78 MO Cav
Seibert, Augustin, 43 Ill Inc
Lieb, Michael, 3 MO Inf
Whitlock, John S., 3 MO Inf
Schmith, Joseph, 78 MO Cav
Kirzner, Lawrentze, 78 MO Inf
Spaekley, Joseph, 78 MO Inf
Heh_, Jacob G., 32 IN Inf
Erautmann, Constantin, 33 MO Inf
Maurice, Bernard, 21 MO Inf
Gremminger, Christian, 47 MO Inf
Schelly, August, MO Inf
Meyer, Jacob, 21 MO Inf
Russel, Frank H. 3 MO Inf, 2 Cal (?) Cav
Herter, Charles A., 8 MO Cav
Will, George, 21 MO Inf
Lachance, August, 47 M Inf
Beergert, Joseph, 8 MO Cav
Bienvenu, Mary formerly widow of Keton, Battire, 68 Col'd Vol
Baumgartner, John, 2 MO Inf
Reubsom, Adam, 78 MO Mtd Inf
Burle, Alexander, 86 MO Inf
Naeth, _nsula widow of Peter Naeth, 86 MO Inf
Muessia, John, 86 MO Inf
Catherine Mussig widow of Karl, Da____, 86 MO Inf
Fanton, Alexander, 15 IL Cav
Hayman, Prululu I., 2 MO Art
Gokerst, Leo A., 2 MO Art
Hurka, Jacob, 4 MO Inf, 15 MO Inf
Fallert, Joseph, 78 MO Inf
Panratown, Leibert, 78 MO Inf
Govro, Moise, No Unit Given

Govro, Carolina widow of Govro, Bernard, No Unit Given
Beauchamp, Michel, No Unit Given
White, John (colored), MO Art
Schaettler, Charles, No Unit Given
Beckermann, George, 30 MO Inf
Schafer, Frederic, 2 MO Inf
Moser, Mary widow of John P. Moser, 11 MO
Ehaumure, Charles, 21 MO Inf
Willis, Joseph C., No Unit Given
Rottler, Valentine, 78 MO Inf
Govro, Felix, No Unit Given
Saint Gem, Hustavus, 47 MO Inf
Courtois, Henry, 21 MO Inf
Mary Gimino widow of John Gimino, 36 IL Inf
Scott, James, 48 MO Inf
Berry, Hiram, 21 MO Inf
Leon Labrier, 47 MO Inf
Frank Kohnr, 13 MO Inf
Nobert Kemph, Mislayed his discharge
Laura Skewes widow of William V. Skewes, 47 MO Inf
Bernhard Klein, 2 MO Heavy Art
Charles Buhl, Confederate, No Unit Given
Ana Vorst widow of Joseph Vorst, 12 MO Inf
Dr. J. Francis Bernags, Hosptial
Henry Stolte, Seaman No. 25 Gov Navy Colassus
John W. Small (Schmal___), 47 MO Inf
Leon Herzog, 2 MO Inf
Louis Lux, Mo State Militia
Jacob Falk, 15 MO Inf
Charles F. Carasow, Surgeon, Sanitary Comm
Mary Valentine widow draws pension but does not know how long he served
John B. Godair, 78 MO Cav
George W. Dorge, 31 MO Inf
Albert Lalemendur, 21 MO Inf
Andrew Kunkel, 53 IL Inf
Franze Oberle, 2 MO Art
Laurence Siebert, 47 MO Inf
Joseph Bader, Mislayed discharge

Paul Huber, 64 MO Inf
John Gessler, 1 MO Inf
Daniel Eller, 1 MO Inf
Charles Schuler, 8 MO Cav
Felix Karl, 100 IL
Frank Beauchamp, 22 Ohio Inf
Maria Bell widow of Charles Beauvaro, 9 Kan Cav
Woods, Dick (Richard), 56 MO Inf
Joseph Blanchet, 1 MO Art
Roman Vogt, 21 MO Inf
George Gattel, 3 MO Inf
Paul Valle, 56 MO Col. Inf
Jacob Kries, Confederate Soldier
Louis Gerards, Confederate Soldier
Christian L. Rath, Sol US
Susan E. widow of St. James, widow Sol US
__. Francis Bernage, Sol US
Annie Hellen, widow Sol US
Edward Reese, Sol US
Andrew Miller, Sol US
Joseph Flice, Sol US
Frank X. Stoll, No Unit Given
Caroline widow of Phillip Joggernut, No Unit Given
Henry H. Hancock, No Unit Given
Bernhard Kist, No Unit given
Mike Stoll, 8 MO Inf
Major Wilkinson, 9 MO Inf
Antoine Briatte, No Unit Given
Conrad Hermann, 8 MO Inf
Katy widow of Henry Otbi, 47 MO Inf
Joseph Tho__re, 21 MO Inf
Richard R. Suderland, 11 MO Inf
Robert U. Halliday, 21 MO Inf
Francis Skenner, 8 MO
Adolpheus Sweek, 47 MO
George _allalory, Confederate, MO
Anton Ron_rtt, 29 NJ
Charles Seibert, 2 MO Lt. Art
Christo Luellfield, 12 MO Inf
Thomas Ma___k, 1 NH Vol
John Pearsail (Tunsail), 50 MO Inf
John Healy, 27 MO Inf
Frank Miller, 2 MO Lt. Art
Frank X. __oetle, 7 MO Inf
William J. Miour, 47 MO Inf
Henry Hosman, 30 IL Vol.
Daniel Rainey, 62 __ Inf
Vincent Steiber, 2 MO Art
August Lentz, 15 MO Inf
Joseph Rusky, 4 MO Inf
William Chandler, No Unit Given
Henry Lanz, No Unit Given
Jacob Mosher, 6 NJ Cav
Leon Boggs, 47 MO Inf

Lawrence Schmiederer, US Sol
William C. Scott, US Sol
Mary Lenz widow of US Sol

Following are very poor quality on microfilm:
James Silvey, 47 MO Inf
John Reitros, 47 MO Inf
Garrot J. Harrelson, 6 IL Cav
Amos Yeager, 27 MO Inf
Richard Petteson, No Unit Given
John W. M_kitt, 22 Ohio Inf
G___ Gabelas, No Unit Given
Lorabell widow of John H. Wachley, 3 MO Cav
Henry Trassbow, 47 MO Inf
Augustus _____ 1 MO Lt. Art
Edward B. Rislein, 5 MO Cav
William _. Byington, No Unit Showing
Job Meadows, No Unit given
Joseph E. Kasher, 6 MO Cav
John Fry, 59 IL Inf

Francis M. Hughes, 3 MO Cav
Geo. H. Griffin, 10 Ohio Cav
John Bryun, 3 Ohio Inf
John W. Reeder, 3 MO Cav
Jule Larsconce (Larscource), US Sol
Andrew Thurman, US Sol
Jno. L. Griffin, US Sol
Wm. R. Resinger, US Sol
Smith, Wm. A., 47 MO Inf
Boyd, J. M., 5 MO Vol
McDaniel, Wm., MO Vol
Homnier, Aarese, 47 MO Vol
Smith, A. M., MO Vol
Dipper, Thomas, 6 MO Vol
Mireus Smith, 10 NY Cav
Cariler, Elej___, 50 IL Inf
Eli S. Heures, 6 IN Inf
Jackson V. McDaniel, 11 MO Inf
Sarah _. Coffee widow of Joshuway Coffee, 117 MO Inf
Sarah J. Allen widow of Areholus V. Allen, 1 MO Lt. Art
Harrey Berry, Confederate, No Unit given
Anderson Counts, 10 MO Cav
Magarat _. Wampler widow of Wm. Wampler, 9 MO vol. Cav
Jacob Wampler, 47 MO Inf
James Pewing, 47 MO Inf
James M. Ferguson, 1 MO Lt Art
John Harrison, 47 MO Vol
Elisha W. Harrison, 47 MO Vol
Wm. F. Brown, 47 MO
Wm. G. Ervin, 14 VA
Francis M. Warniack, 60 MO Inf
Elijah Evans, 14 MO Cav

Jesse Barstow, Confederate, 54 Ark
_____ J. Norman, Confederate, No Unit Given
Linais, G. Couch, No Unit Given
Joseph Ke___bragle, Confederate, No Unit Given
Thomas L. __uerschbrough, No Unit given
Joseph L. Hawthorne, No Unit given
Robert M. Warniack, 50 MO Inf
William Johnson, 8 MO Inf
Malinda Henry widow of Wesley Henry, 6 MO
Richard P. McDonell, Confederate, 8 MO Vol
John S. Beard, Confederate, No Unit Given
Pervis Weiss, No Unit Given
Beurivere dusui Herzurg, No Unit Given
William H. Miller, 47 MO Inf
James W. Watieres, 50 MO Inf
Benjamin F. Henderson, MO Militia
San___J. Barron, No Unit Given
Elizabeth Davis widow, No Unit Given
Lapeold Vager 112 IL Inf
Benhegld Hengleman, 27 MO Inf
Charles Kramer, 27 MO Inf
Andrew Girth, Militia
Peter Vicken, 21 MO Inf
Daniel Loida, MO
Vince Bayer Meci, MO
Valentine Servalet, 2 MO Art
Micheal Servalet, 2 MO Art
Charles Lange, 41 MO
Joisha Billey, 5 NY Inf
William Tucker, MO Inf
James Wallas, 31 MO Inf
John F. Bequett, 18 MO Inf
William Rusad, 47 MO Inf
Henry Weber 22 IA (GA)
William Beckme_, 49 IL
Joseph Sibert, Sol US
Simeon B. Fowler, Sol US
Jacob Leaben, Sol US
Lucinda Pullen, wid Sol US

SCOTT COUNTY MISSOURI

The information below was transcribed from National Archives Microfilm. Occasionally a Confederate name would appear and was lined through. This was a Union Veterans Census. For further information on the Units Listed contact that respective state archives, especially with reference to MO because of State Militia Records and Home Guard records. The National Archives doesn't have those records.

The following abbreviations were used on the microfilm: Lt for light, art for artillery, inf for infantry, cav for cavalry, batt for battalion, MO for Missouri, IL for Illinois, IN for Indiana, Neb for Nebraska, Col for colored, KY for Kentucky, TN and Tenn for Tennessee, PA for Pennsylvania, Vol for volunteer, Ark for Arkansas, Mtd for mounted, Mich for Michigan, Wis for Wisconsin, Sol for soldier, Mis for Mississippi, RC for reserve corps.

NAME/UNIT

Arminta Harrison widow of J.A. Harrison, 2 IL Lt. Art
Augustus C. Rasberry, 50 MO Inf
Chuck Rasberry, 2 IL Lt Art
Jno. D. Clymer, 12 Ten Cav
Joseph T. Anderson, MO Militia
David, Spradlin, 50 MO Inf
Henry P. Mering, 50 MO Inf
Madison Ross, No Unit Given
Joseph Beeckhardt, 7 IL Inf
Morgan A. Bell (Bill), 122 IL Inf
Easter step widow of William Field, No record
Joseph D. Faster (Foster), 22 MO Inf
Larkin M. Hughes, 4 Tenn Cav
George W. Allen, 15 IL Cav
Gotlieb W. Rose, 4 MO Cav
Charles R. Clymer, 50 MO Inf
Wolfgang Weber, 20 MO Inf
Anne Weber widow of John Weber, 29 MO Inf
Ancil Holder, No Unit Given
August LeDore, MO Militia
James C. Clymer, 50 MO Inf
Thos. J. Pool, 50 MO Inf
Elizabeth Bloomberg widow of Louis Bloomberg, 2 IL Lt.Art
Grissilla Gibbs widow of Gibbs, 2 IL Lt Art
Andrew Donaldson, 64 Col Inf
William W. Campbell, 50 MO Inf
Captain Ogden, 60 Col Inf
Mary R. Roden widow of Jno.Roden, 8 MO Cav
William Riley, 56 Col Inf
Sidney Richmond, Confederate, 6 MO Inf
Robert B. Henchon, 57 IN Inf
James Murry, 44 MO Inf
John Dailey, 131 IL Inf
Theo. F. Frazer, No Unit Given
William C. Marshal, No Unit Given
Johnathan B. Torbert, 1 Delaware Cav
Sumtor Forrest, No Unit Given
Elijah M. Oltar, Confederate, 6 MO Inf
Louis Burns, 4 col Art
William A. Waterhouse, No Unit Given
Thomas C. Cooksy, 6 KY Cav
John M. Dunfield, No Unit Given
James. H. Penny, No Unit Given
Samuel H. Clymer, 50 MO Inf
Francis M. Ellis, 56 US Col Inf
Chas S. Smith, 2 IL Art
Watson F. Riggs, 2 KY Cav
George Cavier, US Inf
Mary Vincent widow of Cobble, No Unit Given
William P. Marrs, Kitchens Legion MO Cav
Eliza A. Warren widow of Wm Warren (could be Wasser), Confederate, 12 TN Cav
Rev. Albert G. Horton, Confederate, 13 Ark Inf
John F. Randol, 12 MO Inf
Jacob Row, Confederate, 8 MO Cav
Thomas B. Dodge, 50 MO Inf
James A. Kirkpatrick, Confederate, MO Cav
James N. Malone, Confederate, 5 Tenn Inf
Edward Gibson, 3 Tenn Inf
Missouri F. widow of Samuel Kirkpatrick, Confederate, No Unit Given
Ferdinand Ostner, MSM (MO State Militia), MO Inf
Charles G. Owens, Confederate, Thompsons Unit
Emily C. Peppsins, widow of Allen Williams, Confederate, Thompsons Unit
Lydia E. widow of John C. Warrell, 79 IL Inf
James E. Collins, 3 Ohio Cav
William M. Burke, 12 TN Cav
Enveline widow of Thomas J. Spencer, 83 IL Inf
Ernst Ohmies, MSM, MO Inf
William Gaings, Don't recollect
Archibald P. Land, Confederate, Jeff Thompsons Unit
Charles C. Poe, 15 IL Cav
Washington Trumbo, No Unit Given
Smith Vaughn, 4 TN Cav

Manroe Fulcher, Confederate, 8 MO Cav
Henry Mark__t, 71 IN Inf
Arthur N. Stephens, Confederate, No Unit Given
David Malingly, 6 KY Cav
Granville Stewart, 7 KY Cav
Smith, George W., Confederate, No Unit Given
Ezra H_msson, No Unit Given
Louisa J. widow of Drulh O. Schofield, 33 MO Vol
Forbs, Frank M., No Unit Given
Sarah widow of John Johnson, Confederate, No Unit Given
Deltha C. widow of William A. Darby, Confederate, No Unit Given
Loney, William, Confederate, No Unit Given
Moore, John, 133 IL Inf
Mahulda, widow of F__ck, James W., Confederate, No Unit Given
Wan, Joseph, Confederate, No Unit Given
Shuberry, Allen, Confederate, No Unit Given
Burton, Joseph B., Confederate, 4 TN Cav
Morris, J__rdon, No Unit Given
Mry J. former widow of Good, James M., 10 Tenn Inf
Ousley, Samuel T., Confederate, 1 KY Cav
Stephen H. Wood, 63 IN Inf
William Fisher, 42 IN Inf
William Carpenter, 50 MO Inf
John McKarci, 1 MO Cav
Frank Maxwell, 52 PA Inf
James H. Bradly, No Unit Given
James Copland, 16 IL Cav
Joseph C. Pice, 91 IN Inf
James H. Barnett, 42 IN Inf
John Kenney, 149 IL Inf
James S. Lewis, 1 Neb Inf
Absolum A. Harrison, 4 KY Cav
Thomas B. Scarbrough, 1 Wis Cav
Andrew T. Baker, 12 KY Inf
Christopher C. Hollinsworth, 26 Ohio Inf
James Simpson, 60 IL Inf
William K. Denton, 2 TN Mtd Inf
George C. Reed 143 IN Inf
John G. Bell, 18 IL Inf
B. Jackson Taylor, 31 Tenn Cav
James T. Williams 41 IL Inf
Jeremiah Hardin, 10 Mich Inf
Thomas M. Williams, 9 KY Cav
George W. Scott, No Unit Given
James M. Chadd, 2 KY Art
David Archer, 50 MO Inf
James L. Crow, 31 IL Inf
Nathaniel Arnold, 12 KY Cav
John Squares, No Unit given
Benjamin Thompson, 2 Ten Cav
William M. Jeffords, 50 MO Inf

Samuel Tanner, Sol US detached service
Achan Nuspeay, 49 IL Inf
John H. Cooper, 27 Ohio Inf
Abraham Golson, 87 IL Inf
William H. Black, 1 IL Inf
Ba___ss Johnson, 21 KY Art
Benjamin C. Wilson, 81 IL Inf
Levi Baker, 2 MO Art
Alexander Walker, 5 MO Cav
Joseph H. Williams, 17 IN Inf
Charlotte May widow of Abraham May, 143 IN Inf
George W. Turner, 120 IL Inf
William A. Stovall, 109 IL Inf
Alexander P. Carter, 6 TN Cav
Nehemiah Garrett, 64 IL Inf
John S. Kifer, 29 MO Inf
Joseph Pobst, 2 MO Vol
Davis D. Spradlin, 20 N. LA vol
George L. Crawford, 4 Ohio Cav
Mary Reheart widow, 2 MO Vol
Frank McGrow, 10 MO Vol
Johnithan H. Bryan, 147 IN Vol
James T. Thornton, Confederate, No Unit Given
Plesant G. Prindle, Sol US
Benjamin F. Finley, Sol US
William H. Mitchell, No Unit Given
Roserie Kayhor widow, US Soldier
Mary Holder widow of US Soldier
William G. Kiser, Sol US
John D. Gilespie, Sol US
John Hays, 2 MO Art
Ward L. Smith, ship—Columbia
David J. Crow, 37 IN Inf
Robert W. Walker, 4 Ark
Philip M. Woodruff, 27 KY Inf
Richard H. Mclain, 11 KY Inf
Leonidas D. Nutt, Confederate, 17 Ten Vols
Henry C. Allmon, 30 IL Inf
Thomas T. Hughes 77 IL Cav
Rebuen Smiddy, 60 IL Inf
Stephen W. Underwood, 14 Mis (Wis) Vol
James W. Trimble, 4 MO Inf
Mary Goshe widow of Sam Goshe, MO Home Guard
James K. P. Chewning, 2 IL Art
William Jehun, MO Home Guard
_lvirg J. Chewning widow of A. G. Chewning, 2 IL Art
Andrew Hiebserrer, MO Home Guard
Mathew Sch_oser, MO Home Guard
Jarow Staer, MO Art
Morries Murray, MO Art
Lucien L. Proffit, 15 IL Cav
James K. P. Clawning, Sol US (may be duplicate entry)

Anne E. Clymer widow, No Unit Given
Frank Midelroff, Sol US
Andrew Schoen, MO Home Guard
Celly Bils widow of George Blank, MO Home Guard
Andrew G. Emmerich, No Unit Given
Louis, Hahn, 29 MO cCv
Francis Gouthier, 29 MO Inf
Azargaheth Berger, widow of Adam Berger, MO Home Guard Cav
Alizabeth Essman widow of andrew _. Essman, 50 MO Inf
Louisa Will, widow of James Humphrey, MO State Militia
Crestina S. Ballem widow of Henry Ballm, MO State Militia Cav
Phillips Westrick, State Batt. USRC
Louisa Gastetter widow of Joseph Gastetter, Scott co. Batt. Home Guard US RC
Urrich Glause Scott Batt MO Home guard
Alizabeth Barnberger widow of Wolfson Barnberger, MO Home Guard
Michel Barnberger, MO Home Guard
Charles F. Barnefan, MO Home Guard
John Martin, 50 MO Inf
Thomas C. Adams, MO Malitia Inf
Michian _. Robertson, 29 MO Inf
James W. Compton, 15 KY Cav
Francis F. Hawkins, 7 Mich Cav
Jacob Amar, Cav
Dennie, Die_eve, Cav
Joseph Donne Gariller (Sp-?) Home Guard
Inorz Siebord, 29 MO Inf
Edward Heakam, MO State Militia
Martin Man_, MO Home Guard
Miche LeGrand, MO Home Guard
August Dahogon, MO Home Guard
John B. Scherer, MO Home Guard
Jacob Diebord, MO Home Guard
Catherine Tinene widow of Firehel Tinene, MO Home Guard
Catherine Diebold widow of Peter Diebold, MO Home Guard
Margarett Whitefield widow of William Whitefield
Faroney Scherer widow of Valentine Scherer MO Home Guard
Ferdinan Bisher, IL Art, MO Home Guard
Francis Krantz, MO Home Guard
Catherine Westrick widow of Jacob Westrick, MO Home Guard
Connie M. Heuring wido wof Francis Heuring, MO Home Guard
George Huering, MO Militia
_ George R. Scholz, 1 Neb Inf, 56 ___ Inf
Clemencie J. Hieb___irer, 67 MO Militia

Mary T. Sticke widow of John Stike, 2 MO Inf
Mary Uraine Kieffer widow of Joseph F. Kieffer, MO Home Guard
Charles Velther, MO Home Guard
Louis Buchar, MO Home Guard
Mattan Kampe, MO Home Guard, MO State Militia
George Meine, MO Home Guard
Ferdian Glasseteller, MO HomeGuard, IL Art
Clairborne Sigler, 144 IN Inf
Francis Nations, No Unit Given
Hennery Scholn, MO Home Guard
Jahsi Helm, 48 IL Inf
Firtry Sandiar, 10 MO Cav
Gathail, Johnson, 146 IN Inf
Peter Eckley, 29 MO Inf
Charles Butler, 15 MO, 13 MO cav
Allen Sanders, 50 MO Inf
Vincent Heesler, 18 IL Inf
George Guthrie, 4 MO Cav
Philip Gangle, 13 (MO) Vol
Harve Nuhin, 5 IN Inf
John Powell, 5 Iowa Cav
Martain Sanders, 50 MO Inf
Serah Winchester widow of James Winchester, 50 MO Inf
Elizabeth Miller widow of Joseph Miller, MO Home Guard
Pearl Linal, 4 MO Heavy Art
Margaret Meadin, widow, No Unit Given
August Quillmack, No Unit Given
Adeline More, widow, No Unit Given
Phillip Ruble, Scott Batt Home Guard
Martin Wesmiller, Scott Batt Home Guard
William Rahmoeller, Scott Batt Home Guard
Frank J. Dohagne, Scott Batt Home Guard
Peter Goshe, Scott Batt. Home Guard
Charles Messmer, Scott Batt Home Guard
Julius Albrecht, Scott Batt Home Guard
Josh Messmer, Scott Batt Home Guard
Henry Hillemann, Scott Batt Home Guard
Daniel Eifert, Scott Batt Home Guard
Charles F. Held, Scott Batt Home Guard
John Sunders, Scott Batt Home Guard
David Roth, U S Sol
Henry Peetz, U S Sol
William Lauch, U S Sol
John Schaffer, 2 IL Art
Magdalein Dunning widow of Joseph Dunning, 50 MO Inf
Tter Paetz, (smudged)
Mothere, Rose, (Unknown)
August Klemma, 5 MO Cav
Frank J. Sizers, MO Home Guard
Nucholas Muelter, MO Home Guard

Catherine Thomas widow of Thomas, MO Home Guard
Louisa Messmer widow of Charles B. Messmer, 2 IL Art
James Hiersserer, 2 MO Inf
John Owith, Scott Batt Home Guard
Caroline George widow of Joseph George, Scott Batt Home Guard
Samuel Diebold, Scott Batt Home Guard
Chivenl, Andrew (sp-?) MO State Militia
John Glueck, Scott Batt Home Guard
Laudrence Hoepler, Scott Batt Home Guard
Ravert Finley, 2 IL Art
Andrew Allsman, Scott Batt Home Guard
Charles Ledermann, MO State Militia
Christopher Meinz, 50 MO Inf
Henry A. Meinz, Scott Batt Home Guard
Maxmiliam Brenneron, Scott Batt Home Guard
Charles Hankerson, Scott Batt Home Guard
August Hillerman, Scott Batt Home Guard
Caroline Baneke widow of Charles Baneke, No Unit Given
Henry Musback, Scott Batt Home Guard
Frederick Musback, Merrills Horse
Louisa Westerhold widow of Henry Westerhold, Scott Batt Home Guard
Henry Westerhold, Merrills Horse
Jacob Enderle, Scott Batt Home Guard
Charles Robert, Scott Batt Home Guard
Henry F. Springer, Scott Batt Home Guard
Joseph Bossessmair, Scott Batt Home Guard
Elizabeth A widow of Casore A. Eves, 30 IL Inf
Nancy Jane widow of Robert L. Brown, No Unit Given
Dupore, John R. Confederate, 131 IL Inf
Spraker, John, 30 IL Inf
Louisa G. widow of D. F. Powell, No Unit Given
Skip__an, James, Confederate, No Unit Given
Ellis, Thos. J., Confederate, 6 MO Cav
Parker, John, Confederate, 40 Ark
Martha W. former widow of Frank Chesser, Confederate, No Unit Given
Reddick, Asa _., Confederate 1 Tenn Inf
Morgan, Richard M., Confederate, 2 Louisiana Inf
Sarah C. M. Hanleblueborne widow of Clement Stabler, No Unit Given
Remington, Benj. F., Confederate, 5 TennInf
Stubblefield, W. G. B., Wood's Battalion Inf
D_____, William W., 11 KY Inf
Su_erard, W. J. Confederate, 21 Ark Inf
Helmic Mouser, 3 IL Cav
Anderson, D (J) E. Confederate, 2 MO Cav
Mary Ann widow of Henderson Cantrell, Confederate, No Unit Given
T_ppy, John, Confederate, 7 KY Inf

Ignatius Logel, 29 MO Inf
Christoph Schratte, Scott Batt Home Guard
Daniel Rubel, Scott Batt Home Guard
Wilhelmina Fordenfeld widow of William Fordenfeld, 5 MO Cav
John Rubel, 2 IL Art
John Aug, 4 MO Cav
Frank Weltman, 1 Neb Art
Adam Burger, 10 MO Cav
Jersen Pulley, No Unit Given
Joseph J. Pivmey (Divmey), 29 MO Inf
Mary M. Umnenstall widow of Frederick Umnenstall, Merrills Horse
Constantin Dohogne, 4 MO Cav
John Balattel, No Unit Given
Thomas Pierce, No Unit Given
Martin Tuckmull (sp-?), 3 Mich Cav
William Morgan, Confederate, No Unit Given
William C. Robertson, 6 IL Cav
Ramsey, Harb, 9 MO Inf
Fau_ey R. Ramsey former widow of Samuel W. Miller, Confederate, No Unit Given
Mary A. widow of Ander Ward, No Unit Given
Royd (Boyd), Thomas A. Confederate, Ark
Elizabeth widow of James M. Willis, Confederate, No Unit Given
Crafton, James, W., Confederate, 47 Tenn
Ezekiel York, No Unit Given
Melissa J. widow of Samuel Messer, 35 MO Inf
King Floyd, 14 IL Cav
Lemuel W. Parker, No Unit Given
McCannae, James M. , 21 IN Inf
Pongleton, William B., Confederate, No Unit Given
Peale, Stephen, Confederate, 7 N. Carl Inf
White, W. W. No Unit Given
Curtis, Calvin H., Confederate, 7 KY Inf
Sarah M. Curtis, former widow of David Boyles, 9 IL Cav
Suward, Joseph, 14 MO Cav
Nancy E. widow of A. J. Pigg, No Unit Given
Sparks, William G, 2 MO Inf
Martha widow of James L. Stubbs, Confederate, with Forrest
Duckerson, Louis, No Unit Given
Hale, Charles, 7 Mich Inf
Kemp, Logan, Confederate, No Unit Given
Pool, Colwell P., Confederate, 3 KY Mtd Inf
Adams, James H. Confederate, No Unit Given
Harrell, Thomas H. Confederate, No Unit Given
E_____, William H. 2 MO Lt Art
Hirdge, John W., 3 KY Cav

SHANNON COUNTY MISSOURI

Parts of this census were very bad. I made an attempt to identify as many letters as possible in the names, but in some cases there was just nothing to be seen. However, in some cases the unit was perfectly clear.

The following abbreviations appeared: Inf for infantry, Cav for cavalry, Art for artillery, lt. for light, Sol and Sold for soldier, Vol for volunteer, R for reserve, C for colored, Mtd for mounted, MO for Missouri, IL for Illinois, IN for Indiana, Tenn and Ten for Tennessee, Pa and Penn for Pennsylvania, KY for Kentucky, Kan for Kansas, Corpse for Corps, Ark for Arkansas, Neb for Nebraska, NY for New York, Wisc and Wis for Wisconsin, Ala for Alabama, WV for West Virginia, Miss for Mississippi, Va for Virginia, and Mich for Michigan

NAME/UNIT

Theodore D. Raymond, 7 IL Inf
Jake Faircorut, 175 Ohio Inf
Reuben Ayeten (Ageten), 1 Mich Eng
Eleager Dallus, 48 IL Inf
David M. Jobon, 111 IL Inf
Thomas H. Kenwrothy, 8 MO Cav
William Buffington, 188 Penn Inf
Henry H. Stinnet, 9 Tenn Cav
Edwin _. _recker, US Corpse
Andrew Bridger, 11 Iowa Inf
John G. Edwards, 183 Ohio Inf
Dames M. Carr, 32 MO Inf
Alexander Qualls, 6 IL Cav
Stephen E. Ringer, 15 MO Cav
Frelering E. Barns, 5 Kan Cav
William C. McNeal, 32 IL Inf
Edwin A. Cole, 83 Penn Inf
Collumbus Johnson, 46 MO Inf
William W. Anderson, 152 IL Inf
Albert L. Raymond, 7 Ohio Inf
Sarah H. widow of William Estes, 14 IL Inf
Allen G. T Gray, 13 IL Cav
John R. Wallace, 8 MO Cav
Andrew H. Banister, 2 Ark Cav
Henry Hoops, KY Inf
Louis Rose, 87 IL Inf
George McBride, 14 IN Inf
James C. Younger, 46 MO Inf
Joseph Hart, 197 Ohio Inf
Sarah J. widow of James Crabtree, 2 Neb Cav
David McKinney, 47 IL Inf
William J. Orr, 32 MO Inf
William Ryne, 30 IL Inf
James K. Vanhoosier, 48 MO Inf
James H. Cook, 7 Tenn Inf
Alexander G. Mattox, 25 IL Inf
Henry C. Dawes, 1 Ohio Art
Andrew L. Ladd, 9 KY Cav
John Donahue, 15 IL Inf
John W. Jones, 3 NY Cav
Edward Goodwin, 26 IN Inf
William Sweeney, Sol US
John F. Flood, Sol US
James K. Hutchinson, Sol US
William Watkins, Sol US
Joseph L. Worsham, Sol US
Bartley H. Rich, Sol US
Frank Moran, Sol US
James O'Kelly, Sol US
David Bunch, Sol US
John Jones, 48 IL Inf, 59 US Col Inf, 98 IL Inf, 61 IL Inf
Francis J. Runnels widow of William H. Runnels, 6 MO Cav
J.C. Kelso, 73 Ohio Inf
Elizabeth widow of Thomas Shelton, Inf
Joshua K. Farrar, MO Inf
_____ R. widow of _____ Shane, No Unit Given
Benjamin Welch, US Sol
James J. McMillen, US Sol
Joseph Skillin, US Sol
Duniven, William L., 32 MO Inf
Coats, William B., 3 MO Cav
John L. C. Richards, 124 IL Inf
Sarah Foshe, 8 Ten Inf
James L. Allstr_____, 9 Ten Cav
Thomas J. Keith, 81 IL Inf
Louise Justice wife of William Justice, No Unit Given
Francis J. Banks widow US Sol
Jacob Yates, 78 Ohio
James Fulks, 21 KY
John Hurst, 26 MO
Patrick H. Todd, 16 KY
Purcive B. Lambert, 21 KY
Sara C. Layman widow of Joseph F. Layman, MO

Lydia A. Odom widow of William R. Odom, No Unit Given
Samuel A. Reese, 2 Tenn Inf
Eli Beller, 11 KY Inf
Francis M. Shelton widow of _____ Shelton, 3 MO Cav
William M. Killough., 149 IN Inf
Joseph Killin, 120 IL Inf
Elizabeth Anderson widow of John Anderson, 60 IL Inf
Catherine Malone former widow of John B. James, No Unit Given
Joseph R. Shrewsberry, 13 MO Cav, 5 MO Cav
Larue, James Michael, 2 MO Art
Grantham, Allen J. 31 IL Inf
Richardson, Milferd E. Hall Ga____ Battalion
Brown, John J., 86 NY Inf, 1 NY Cav
John A. Embeck, Soldier, Sailor
Jas. K. Kirkpatrick, Soldier
William R. Yearwood, No Other Info Given
Emaline Morman widow of Will Golder
Joseph G. Pettit, Sold
Levi Young, Sold
Haliday, David K. 128 IL Inf
Rodebush, George W., 86 IL Inf
Edgar, William R. 63 MO
Edward W. Moore alias Edward W. Ke____e, 22 Pa Vol-R
Elizabeth Jarrett widow of Jarrett, Thomas, No Unit Given
Amera Burrell widow of George W. Burrell, 40 IL Inf
James Odle, 122 IL Inf
Butt, John D., 38 MO Vol
Powell, William H., 11 MO Cav
Chafin, Franklin M., 7_MO, East MO Militia
Gussin, Andrew J., 13 Wisc Inf
Austin, Moses, MO Cav
Phebe A. Griffith widow of Samuel (Lamuel) P. Griffith, No Unit Given
Youngblood, William R., 145 IL Inf
Sumter, Ruben V., Light Art
Fisher, Milel, 14 IL Cav
John Frakes alias John K. Frakes, IL Inf
John W. Taylor alias William Davis, 10 IL Cav
John Thurman, 6 MO Cav
Comley, Vernon R., 131 IN Cav
Louisa A. Huffman former widow of John Barton, MO
Huffman, John, No Unit Given
House, John, 120 IL Inf
Morman, Simeon S., 8 MO Cav
Naillus, John B., MO Vol
H_gorn, Joseph, 1 MO Vol
Hester J. Patterson widow of Joseph Patterson, 6 MO Cav

Davis, William B., 48 MO Vol
Sherrill, Silas W., 13 IL Cav
Weaver, Thomas J., No Unit Given
Morris, John W., 47 MO
Glasener, Jessie P., 5 IL Cav
Garrett, Almasine, KY Home Guard
Hess, William R., 60 IL Inf
Monroe, William A., 2 IN Cav
Sayne, Zachariah J., Independent Rangers, Taxas & Pulaski
Doronard, Stephen, No Unit Given
McKutt___, David, 2_5 PA Inf
Edwards, Daniel T., US Navy 3 Division
Pike, William G., 1 Ala Cav, 42 IL Inf
Anderson, Providence, 6 WV Inf
Brewington, Thomas, 1 Tenn Inf
Huntley, James, US Marshal
Anderson, Vincent, 48 IL Inf
Kirkpatric, Joseph, No Unit Given
Brown, Christopher, 50 IN Inf, 5 KY Cav
Needer, Leadner O., US C. Inf
Elizabeth Anderson widow of John M. Anderson, 60 IL—entry crossed out Confederate
Hasler, Charles R., No Unit Given
Craig, Willilam H., 48 MO Inf
Spurgin, James H., 33 Iowa Inf
Watts, Robert W., 16 Wis Inf
Nelson, John B., 10 Tenn Inf
Simmons, Willie B., 32 MO Inf
Kell, John, 32 MO Inf
Rogers, Joseph A. 85 IN Inf
Prater, David M., 5 Tenn Cav
Hatch, Sylvester E., 2 IL Cav
Harrison, William M., 47 MO Inf
Wells, John C., 63 MO Militia
Carpenter, Green B., 2 Ark Cav
Endy, James,15 IL Cav
Duer, William, MO Vols.
Lanham, Berry H., 31 MO Inf
Needham, Ferdinand C., 3 MO Cav
Thompson, John, 5 MO Cav
Sulivan, William R., 5 MO Cav
Bounds, Rufus M., 33 MO Inf
Sarah Thompson widow of Lane (Louie) Thompson, Sol

Next entries are very poor or not legible, however unit designation was clear for most part
Lambert H. Charles, 131 IL
Ferdinand, Thomas W. 17 Ohio
George Raymond,75 Ohio
NOT LEGIBLE, WIDOW, 78 OHIO
NOT LEGIBLE, 52 KY
NOT LEGIBLE, 78 OHIO
NOT LEGIBLE, 75 OHIO

____WIDOW OF CULLEN, ERNST W., 23

FINNEY, E____, 1ST VA CAV
CARR, _____ 10 OHIO CAV
ROS__, FULTON, 5 VA CAV
_____, DAVIS M. , 97 MO INF
FRIPP, EVAN H., 31 MO INF
LOMBARD, JULIAN _., TEN CAV
NOT LEGIBLE, 26 MICH
NOT LEGIBLE, MO
NOT LEGIBLE
_____REEVES, 29 MO
NOT LEGIBLE, 63 IL
NOT LEGIBLE, 63 IL
NOT LEGIBLE, MO
NOT LEGIBLE, 14 OHIO INF
_____A. MOZART, WIDOW OF CHARLES
KESERB____, 41 OHIO INF
ELIZABETH CREPPS, No Unit Given
Dr. arper A. M_ery, No Unit Given
Thomas Wright, 31 MO Inf
Robert Bragg, 18 IL Inf
Henry Heiney, 14 Iowa Inf
Christopher C. Moore, 13 KY Cav
Edward C. Ballick, No Unit Given
Francis M. Stevens, 41 IL Inf
William L (F.) League, 13 Ohio Inf
George W. Dewoody, 64 IL Inf
Lorenzo D. Pendland alias Lornzo D. McLean, 1 Miss Mtd. Rifles
Charity Sinclair, widow of James Sinclair, 3 MO Cav
Elizabeth M. Gates widow of William Gates, No Unit Given
Beverly M. Stubblefield, 125 IN Cav
James M. Crabtree, 11 MO Cav
John T. (L.) Henskey (Huskey), No Unit Given
Joseph W. Adams, 50 IN Inf
Peter Link, 111 NY Inf
Nancey widow of George W. Bailer, 33 KY Inf
King, William, 8 KY Inf
Lancaster, Samuel S., 110 IL Inf
Thomas J. Rowlett, Sol
Sarah E. Creger widow, Sol
Leoing Gibbs, widow SOL

STODDARD COUNTY MISSOURI

The following abbreviations were used: IL for Illinois, Penn and PA for Pennsylvania, Mich for Michigan, MA for Massachusetts, Ken and KY for Kentucky, Kan for Kansas, IN for Indiana, Tenn for Tennessee, Wis for Wisconsin, Ala for Alabama, NY for New York GA for Georgia, Miss for Mississippi, Ark for Arkansas, and LA for Louisiana.   Cav for cavalry, Inf for infantry, Ind for independent, col for colored, vol for volunteer, lt for light, art for artillery, sol for soldier, regt for regiment, eng for engineer, grds for Guards, mtd for mounted, Mid for middle, Batt for battery.

Parts of this census were so very faint. I attempted to find as many of the letters in the name as possible as well as a military unit.

NAME/UNIT

Jams Johnson, discharged by man from home
William J. Palmer, 15 IL Cav
John H. Harris, 97 Penn Inf
Mary E. Bateman former widow of Alexander Srirke, 131 IL Inf
George W. Slankard, 13 IL Cav
Charlotte Lewis widow of James Lewis, discharge lost
Lawson Rhoads, 29 Mich Inf
Margaret Schrader widow of Riley Ridge, 140 MA Inf
Thomas Pry, 58 VA Ind Inf
Thomas J. Stafford, 79 MO Cav
John W. Newman, 8 Ken Cav
Sarah C. Steward widow of Samuel Stewart, 2 IL Cav
Ava S. Pierce widow of John Pierce, 15 IL Cav
Dicey Baily widow of Thomas Patterson, discharge lost, lady can tell nothing
Martin Hart, 4 Tenn Inf
Cornelius Williamson, 9 IL Inf
John Mitchell, 3 IL Inf
John W. Stewart, gone from home discharge locked in safe place, is pensioner
Alexander O. Scots, 53 IN Inf
William L. Tilman, 110 IL Inf
Thomas Land, 14 MO Cav
Houstin Dillyard, 12 MO Cav
James J. Hampton, 1 Iowa Cav
William Bruckman, 16 MA Inf
Nucholas G. Natiur (Natins), 2 IL Inf
Jessee Janison, ?_ Cav
Henry Heatley, 47 MO Inf
Giles J. Natins, 2 IL Inf
Ebenezer Jones, 2 Col Cav
James Sturgis, 13 Ken Cav
William Hawk, 27 IL Cav
William W. Sicles, 5 MO Vol Inf

Martha F. widow of William A. Stewart, 3 MO Cav
Susan E. Henson, widow, no unit given
John L. White, Sol., no unit given
Diana, J. Jordan, widow, no unit given
Penelopy Throwr, widow, no unit given
Rhoda Holleck, widow, no unit given
Amanda Henson, widow, no unit given
George M. Highsom, soldier, no unit given
Lawson Proffer, militia for 12 weeks
Daniel Green, 38 IL Inf
Thomas Tanner, 31 IL Inf
Martin Tropt (Trost), 50 MO Inf
Martha R. Ing, 40 IL Inf
John M. Shirley, 13 IL
George Adams, 49 IL Inf
James M. Millstead, 11 MO Inf
Thomas C. Welch, 50 MO Inf
Sidney Casey, 18 IL Inf
John F. Reese, 2 MO Cav
Hary R. Tyson, 2 Ohio Inf
Chris Ulrich, no unit given
Francis M. Allen widow of Allen, 6 IL Cav
Nancy Asrar(sp?) widow of Martin Hefner, 29 MO Inf, 32 MO Inf
Stephen Looney, US Sol
Susan Collins, Sol widow
Zeralda Yates, Sol widow
Alonzo D. C. Laughley, US Sol
Emily Hefner, Sol widow
Jacob Beard, US Sol
Tony McGee, US Sol
Clayton T. Huntington, US Sol
William W. Swith, US Sol
Louis J. Bodine, US Sol
____ Browning, No Unit Given
Baltimore Taylor (col), No Unit Given
M.L. Crabtree, 50 MO Inf
James Reynolds, 6 Tenn Cav
Charles Hargrave, No Unit Given
Joseph H. Johnson, No Unit Given

John A. Young, 6 Tenn Cav
William Wilson, 8 MO State Militia
Thomas _____, 6 MO Cav
Norman B. Fellers, 47 IL Inf
William C. Nearby, 2 MO State Militia
George S. Kitchen, 5 MO State Militia
Sarah late widow of Christian Joseph Shrum, 3 MO Cav
Anna Obards widow of Collumbus Obards, 13 MO Inf
Sarah E. Nash widow of Isaac Nash, 29 IL Inf
George W. Brill, 29 IL Inf
Dennis Harly, 2 MO State Militia Cav
Moss Marcum, 1 Tenn Cav
William J. Kitchen, 6 MO Cav
Samuel P. Curd, 50 MO Inf
Zacharia Goforth, 1 IN Cav
Abigail Gillespie widow of John Gallispie, 9 KY Inf
Phineas Bunton, 136 ___ Inf
Livingston Scholar, 2 MO State Militia
Jasper A. Bullard, 6 IL Cav
Henry Willson, 4 KY Inf
James G. Crump, 2 MO State Militia Cav
Layfayette Cortney, 14 IL Inf
Charles Tarfang, 110 IL Inf
Henry W. Martin, 12 Mich Inf
William H. Story, 5 MO State Militia Cav
Maberry Rigges, 50 MO Inf
James Ary, 50 MO Inf
Harrison Duglis, 6 MO Cav
Michael Halt, 6 Ten Cav
John M. Herero, 3 MO Cav
Alexander Patterson, 5 MO Cav
Orvile F. Thomas, 8 Tenn Inf
Alford N. Gray, 48 KY Inf
James J. Akers, 154 IL Inf
William H, Singleton, 1 MO Heavy Art
John Luffey, 5 MO State Militia
Wm. L. Fagan, Soldier
James Grant, Soldier
Livingston Scholes, Soldier
Wm. Stanley, Soldier
Sarah Ray, widow Soldier
John C. Helderman, Soldier
Margaret Bailey widow Soldier
James O. Williams, Soldier
Adelia Hallis, widow Soldier
Mayberry Riggs, Soldier
C.N. Summers, Soldier
Pryor Daniel, Soldier
Seism, Samuel, 2 IL Art
Christian James, 101 Iowa Inf
Seism, George, 2 IL Art
Felker, George W. 3 KY Cav
Jones, Anartis L., 29 IL Inf

Elizabeth Norman formerly widow of Taylor, John A., 12 MO State Militia Cav
Smith, Malartha former widow of Buchanan, Daniel A., 7 Tenn Cav
Ponis, William L., 146 IL Inf
Batchelor, George M., 2 MO State Militia Cav
Goodin, James H., 12 MO State Militia Cav
Stavey, Hirmam H., 29 IL Inf
Kitche, Reuben, 13 MO Cav
Gregory, Alexander, 11 IL Cav
Taylor, David N., 9 KY Cav
Bacon, William A. 2 MO Cav, 14 MO Cav
Jackson, John, 13 TN Cav
Linard, Lavinier widow of Linard, Joseph, 2 MO Cav
Hill, Caroline widow of Hill, James W., 80 IL Inf
Wheeler, William, 60 IL Inf
Crews, Isaac H., 2 MO State Militia, 14 MO Cav
Green, James M., 87 IL Inf
Jones, Benjamin F., 8 KY Inf, 4 KY Mtd Inf
Bradshaw, Manda formerly widow of Bess, Lawson M., 5 MO State Militia Cav
Davis, Presley L., 2 Ohio Cav
Proffer, Logan, 5 MO State Militia Cav
Coffman, Winters P., 133 Ohio Inf
George Briton, 19 US Inf
Missouri E. Edrington, US Sol widow
Lucinda Goodman, US Sol widow
Edmond Foster, US Sol
Mahala P. West, US Sol widow
Millington N. Abernathy, Confederate, No Unit Given
Charles H. Bashame, Confederate, MO Cav
Beu S. Butler, 29 IL Vol
Joseph Howell, Confederate, Kitchen's Regiment
Thomas M. Crain, 81 IL Inf
Henry H. Bedford, 1 MO Cav
William C. Cole, 71 IL Vol
Nancy Sykes widow of Henry Sykes dec'd, No Unit Given
Thomas J. Sifferd, 50 MO Inf
Jane Harty (Hasty) widow of Greenbery Hosty (decd), No Unit given
James E. Boyd, 7 MO Cav
John Cantrell, 31 MO Inf
Robert Fortius, 9 IL Vol
Harriett Franklin former widow of Green Adkins, No Unit Given
Nancy J. Young late widow of Jesse F. McNeal, No Unit Given
Susan Williams late widow of David Moore, 18 IL Inf
John C. Sick, No Unit Given

Martha M. Montgomery widow of Major General Montgomery, 6 MO Cav
John M. Stephens, 50 MO Vol
Elizabeth Culbertson widow of James Culbertson, Confederate, No Unit Given
Courtney Webb widow of James Webb dec'd, 60 IL Vol
Shadrack S. Lackey, 42 Ala Inf
Jacob Cossart, 8 MO Cav
William M. Rankins, No Unit given
James Patterson, 2 IL Lt. Art
Lavinia Pruett widow of Isaac Pruett, 144 IN
Elizabeth Triplett late widow of Jacob Brown, No Unit Given
Henry S. Blocker, NoUnit Given
Geroge A. DeBume (sp?), 10 IL Inf
Thomas W. Greenlead, 2 MO Cav
Alexander D. McWilliams, Confederate, 1 KY
Thomas J. Stafford, 50 MO Vol
John A. Snider, Confederate, No Unit Given
Taylor Sisk, Confederate, No Unit Given
William R. Williams, Confederate, No Unit Given
Susan E. Bolin, late widow of William J. Bolin, No Unit Given
John V. McIlvey, 2 MO Cav
Samuel Robes, No Unit Given
Orson B, Layton, No Unit Given
John W. Brown, Conederate, Geo. Cockerd's Regt
Mary C. Culbertson late widow of Jesse Gibson, No Unit Given
Mary J. Triplett late widow of Abner Triplett, Confederate, J.S. Marmaduke's Company
James C. Eaves, Confederate, No Unit Given
William J. Bolin, Confederate, Col. Jeffers Company
William H. Crosson, 42 IL Inf
King F. Kirby, Confederate, Hick's Company
George W. Nichols, 71 Ohio Vol
Joseph H. Wells, 96 NY Inf
James D. Carter, Confederate, No Unit Given
William. A. (R.) Harper, Confederate, No Unit Given
Chester Combs, 62 IL Cav
Edward R. Cunningham, Confederate, No Unit Given
William D. Watts, 4 IL Cav
Reuben A. S_____ton, 148 IL Inf
Felix Timmons (Sp?), Confederate, 8 KY Inf
John H. Harper, Confederate, No Unit Given
Martha A. Cole widow of Elihue W. Cole, Captain, No Unit Given
John F. Aslin, Confederate, 12 KY
William C. Wilson, Confederate, No Unit Given
Nicholas M. Willis, Confederate, No Unit Given

Elisha H. L_____ius, Confederate, 6 MO Cav
Isaac Ma_er, Confederate, 2 MO Inf
Virgil R. Embry, 11 KY vol
Framcis M. C__nbs, 70 IL Vol
John C. Maberry, KY vol
Aaron Lusk (Luck), No Unit Given
Amandia Harvey, widow, 12 MO vol
Hunter, Foster, 6 MO Cav
Christian, William, 2 MO Cav
Majors, Pleasant W., 12 MO Cav
Johnson, William A., Confederate 5 MO Inf
Ballard, Jesse, Confederate, 9 MO Cav
Riesse, Henry, 1 MO Art
Jones, Eli, 5 MO Inf
Link, Daniel, 50 MO Inf
Walker, Alexander, 12 KY Inf
Walker, Ephraim, 14 MO Cav
Sarah W. widow of Morrman, William, M., 79 MO Inf
Story, Henderson, 2 MO Inf
Skelton, John B. 32 MO Inf
Crawford, Eldridge, 50 MO Cav
Palmer, Benjamin, 15 IL Inf
Elmore, William T., 22 Tenn Inf
Bolick, George, 5 MO Cav
Walton, Jeremiah, 5 Iowa Cav
Bryant, George, 15 IL Cav
White, James M., 17 KY Cav
Poe, James, 5 MO Cav
Poe, Terry, 12 MO Cav
Jeroldt, Louis C., Eng Little Giant Granger
Hopkins, Wiley, 50 MO Inf
Robinson, Elijah, Confederate, 18 GA Inf
Casey, Joseph L., Confederate, 40 GA Inf
Timmons, J. Garet, KY Cav
Herndon, Madison, Confederate, 23 Tenn Inf
McDowell, Thomas J., 5 MO Cav
Glover, Frederic J., 12 MO Cav
Davis, James G., 15 Tenn Inf
Miller, Henderson, 50 MO Inf
Baker, Joseph, 7 MO Cav
Hearse, Lain____, Confederate, 1 Tenn Inf
Smith, Amos, 31 IL Inf
McCla___, Thomas B., 1 MO Cav
Herman, Benjamin, 143 IN Inf
Alvis, Richard J., 1 US Inf
Estes, Henry t., 5 MO Inf
Hill, Edward, 1 Ala Cav
Horn, Charles C., MO Inf
McFarland, William A., MO Cav
Charles Peters, Sol
John J. Parks, Sol
John M. Allen, Sol
William _. Kelly, Sol
John _. McDonel, 5 NY Cav
Chas. L. Taylor, 1 KY Art

Isaac Urrich, 93 PA Vol
Ezekiel Reed, 47 IN Vol
Wm. P. Smith, 113 IL
Laura E. Benson, widow US Sol, No Unit Given
Theodore L. Sharrard, 148 IN
James Reynolds, No Unit Given
John C. McGee, 56 IL
Levi Hatchett, No Unit Given
D. L. Shirk, 9 IL Inf, 3 IL Cav
Nathan B___dle, 8 IN Cav
Fannie Smith wid of James W. Smith, No Unit Given
Wm. Strang, 50 Ohio
Mary H. Porter widow of Wm. H. Porter, No Unit Given
Margaret Buford widow of Wm. Buford, No Unit Given
F____ De Journett, 58 IN
James Eav__g, 13 KY Inf
Joseph Brooks, No Unit Given
Clara Johnson widow of Calvin Johnson, 50 MO
James Dalton, 6 IL Cav
Julius C. Morgan, 35 IL
John M. Pasley, 2 IL Cav
Chas. Allen, 1 Mich, 5 US Vol
Moses Welles, 2 MO Art
Wm. J. Butts, No Unit Given
Robt. W. Thompson, 50 MO Inf
Annie Hickman widow of Berry Hickman, No Unit Given
Thornt England, No Unit Given
Robt. A. Haris, 7 IL, 2 Tenn
James M. Young, MO State Militia
James A. Dodd, 7 KY grds
Chauncey Vandougen, 50 Wisc
Geo. W. Thompson, 58 IN
Wm. A. Booths, 68 IN
Wm. A. Thompson, MO State Militia, 50 MO
James D. Mansker, No Unit Given
Geo. W. Culbertson, 7 Kan Vol
Chas. McGuire, 49 IL Inf
Thos. M. Pasley, 2 IL Cav
Adam C. McCormick, 129 IN
Wm. A. Vinson, MO State Militia
Wm. A. McQuay, 87 IL
Martha E. Lawrence widow of Abraham Lawrence, No Unit Given
Mary J. Pattrick widow of Nathan Pattrick, No Unit Given
Greenville Howe, 28 IN Cav
John Vinson, 29 MO
James L. Gregory, 87 IL
Geo. W. Walton, 18 IN
Geo W. Ellis, 7 Kan Cav
George Morgan, No Unit Given
Berry, Sarah A., widow US Sol

Shaffer, Theobalt, US Soldier
Morgan, George, US Sol
Wood, William, 6 IL Cav
Lyon, George W., 11 IL Inf, 109 IL Inf
Michael, Frederic N., Confederate 1 Miss Inf
Boyt, Elisha t., 60 IL Inf
Charles P. Clark, Sol US
Henry V. Matlock, Sol US
John J. McKimmamon, Sol US
Isaac H. Conner, Sol US
Evan E. Arnold, Sol US
James T. Garner, Sol US
Thomas N. Tate, Sol US
William Irving, Sol US
Salomon Simmons, Sol US
Jarrett Tramble, Sol US
George A. Bartlett, Sol US
Robert M. Barnes, Sol US
Giles H. Shehorn, Sol US
Lipsey James, 110 IL Inf
Mary M. widow of Brown, Thomas B., Delaware Inf
Mary M. widow of Neely, Hiram S., Tenn Inf
Swinsrey, Jesse C., 15 KY Inf
Cinda widow of M. Lord, No Unit Given
Tatissn, Shepard B., 50 MO Inf
Young, William J. IL Inf
Bryan, Jasper, 152 IL Inf
Woodard, James, 50 MO Inf
Anthony, William, 7 Penn Inf
Greene, Marion, 81 IL Inf
Bartley (Hartley), William F. No Unit Given
Whittaker, Alexander, 11 Ken Inf
Bailey, Columbus D. 1 MO Cav
Smith, James, 128 IL Cav
Nolen, Thomas J., 143 IL Inf
H____, Lonzo C., 9 NY Heavy Art
Nancy G. widow of Mitchell, John P., 17 KY Cav
Snell, John R., 1 MO Cav
Wilson, John, 13 IN Inf
Little, Gow_, IN
Moore, John N. 5 Iowa Cav
Allen, William D. No Unit Given
Martin, William, MO Cav
Rourke, John, IL Inf
Hall, John, Ohio Inf
Bradfuehrer, John C., Ohio Inf
Deming, James H., 81 IL Inf
Manzy, William S., 11 KY Inf, 35 MO
Downey, Alfred, 43 IL Inf
Boughton, George N., 78 NY Inf
Sarah widow of York, William A., 18 IL Inf
Sarah widow of Joseph Bridges, 60 IL Inf
Landes, James E., 80 IL Inf
Garner, Jeremiah, 12 MO Cav

Garner, Eli J., 5 MO Inf
Stewart, John W., 31 IL Inf
Mary widow of Fields, Abraham, 31 IL Inf
Adams, Jeremiah, No Unit Given
Crawford, Josiah, 63 IN Inf
Deason, Amon, 120 IL Inf
Keer, Charles L., 33 IL Cav
Wright, Joseph H., 13 IN Inf
McLean, Lewis, 87 IL Inf
Parks, Christopher C., 5 KY Cav
Hoffman, Joseph, 8 US Inf
Marshall, Alfred, 113 IN Inf
Miller, James(Jones), 23 Mich Inf
Stricklin, James W., 2 MO Inf
Car__er, John C., 153 IL Inf
F___rr, D__d__us, 3 MO State Militia
Evans, James W., 3 MO State Militia
Fields, Benjamin R., 43 IL Inf
P___d___r, Charles E., 2 MO Inf
Butler, John W., 26 Ala Inf
Gibson, Riley, 25 IN Inf
Higgins, William H., 9 IL Inf
H___t, John A., 12 KY Cav
Smith, William I., 7 Kan Cav
Duncan, William T., Confederate, 8 Ark Inf
Sevier, John M., 18 Ohio Inf
Laster, Jonathan, 2 MO Cav
Smith, Rufus, Confederate, MO Inf
O'Hare, Patrick 8 MO Inf
Willow, Moris B., Confederate, 5 MO Cav
Hopper, William T., 4 Tenn Inf
Lambert, Henry C., Confederate, MO Inf
Taylor, Henry B. Confederate, 2 MO Cav
Rowdy, Charles, Confederate, 6 MO Inf
Birchfield, Henry A., Confederate 2 MO cav
Cunningham, Alexandria, Confederate, 2 MO Inf
Stewart, Robin C., 5 MO Cav
Howell, Elijah, Confederate, 7 MO Cav
Mobley, Patricia widow of Mobly, Francis M., 29 IL Inf
Hulda widow of _____, James, 2 MO State Mil Cav
Fields, James, 2 MO Inf
Foster, John A., 2 Ark Cav
_____, James M., 31 IL Inf
_arol Elina widow of Hicks, Se_riore, 1 Ala Cav
Potter, Leander widow of Robert Potter, 25 Ark Inf
Edwards, Thomas J., Confederate 12 MO Cav
Robertson, Francis, 48 KY Cav
Patterson, Caladeria widow of William J.
Patterson, Confederate, MO Inf
R____, Jonathan, Confederate, 1 MO Inf
Lambert, Thomas J., 2 IL Cav
Hart, John, 6 IL Cav
Maloney, Patrick, 29 IL Inf

Maize, Jesse W., 1 Miss Cav
Anderson, George W., 47 MO Cav
Moore, Polley widow of Moore, H_bel E., 11 IL Cav
Arch, Matthews, 110 IL Inf
Ridle, James R., Confederate, 1 MO Cav
Cooper, Jarvis (James) C., Confederate, 3 MO Cav
Grotehouser, James P., 9 IL Inf
Neld, William T., 56 Ohio Cav
_____, Joseph H. 56 IL Inf
Hamilton, David H., Confederate, 2 MO Inf
Cunningham, Jarvis (James) F., Confederate 8 Ark Inf
Reese, James P., Confederate, 8 MO Cav
Sadler, Monroe J., Confederate 8 MO Cav
Robinson, William H., Confederate 21 Miss Inf
Trobridge, Albert A., 111 IL Inf
Smith, Edney P., Confederate 5 Tenn Inf
Proffer, William F. 50 MO Inf
Graham, Sarah A. widow of Graham, James M. Confederate—Ohio Inf
Miller, Isaac, 2 MO Cav
Smith, Henry W., 5 KY Cav
Hartline, Henry W., 18 IL Inf
John R. Williams, 52 IN Inf
J.A. Middling, 6 IL Cav
John Sutter, 39 IL Inf
Charles Gibson (colored), 9 LA Inf
Malissa A. widow of Andrew J. Fager, 105 PA Inf
William Frey, 9 IL Inf
George Newman, 6 IL Cav
Sarah E. McMurty formerly widow of John D. Simpson, No Unit given
D. S. Stephens, 33 Iowa Inf
Dennis Harty, 2 MO State Mil Cav
David H. Settles, US Sol
Susan Smith, widow US Sol
Martha H. Dodson, widow US Sol
Mary A. Fellhouse widow of James Sulivant,
James W. Mangum, Cou & US
James J. Edmonson, enrolled in MO Militia
Harrison Allen, 29 MO Inf
William Odonald, 31 IN Inf
Amos Depart, 97 IN Inf
Mary Johnson widow of Moris B. Johnson, 129 IL Inf
George Harbin, 97 IN Inf
Charles Dillard, 131 IL Inf
Russell Cagteel, 8 Tenn Inf
Catherine Boyer wdow of Trunnell Boyer, 91 IN Inf
James H. Goforth, 1 IL Cav
William R. Kitchen, 12 MO State Militia Cav, 5 MO State Militia Cav

William H. Huff, 29 IL Inf
N. E. Dysart, 57 IN Inf
Thomas C. Campbell, 118 IN Inf, 143 IN Inf
Byrl Williams, 76 Ohio
Carrol Harty, 2 MO State Militia Cav
Sarah E. widow of Robert W. Carpenter, 48 KY inf
W. F. Williams, 80 IN Inf
Mary J. Phoenin widow of John W. Atkinson, 6 Tenn Cav
Asnenia Buchanan formerly widow of Robert Rogers, No Unit Given
J.W. Smith, 29 MO Inf
Amanuel Decker, not at home and wife could give nothing, No Unit Given
Andrew L. Meadows, 98 IL Inf
Jessee Boyce, 13 IL Cav
Aaron J. Grammer, 109 IL Inf
William J. Way., 1 Mid. Tenn Inf
Peter Ely, 9 Ohio Cav
William A. King, 87 IL Mtd. Inf
Joseph Harris, 2 IL Lt. Art
William U.(N.) Cook, 19 Ohio Inf
Sinie Bresher wid of Jessee Bresher, 59 IN Inf
Henry T. Watson, 39 OH Inf
William Wilkerson, 155 IL Inf
Leonard Duncan, 8 IL Inf, Alton Batt 100 Day Inf
Zachariah Sinks, 60 IL Inf
John Stevens, 32 IL Inf
Andrew J. Mathis, 12 KY Cav
W. P. B_kers, 50 IN Inf
Joseph Williamson, 29 IL Inf
James McGowen, 37 IL Inf
Alexander Melton, IN Inf
Francis M. Williams, 56 IL Inf
T.J. Rittenburry, 3 IL Cav
Elisha Sanders, 60 IL Inf
William Stringer, 12 MO Cav
Nancy Thomas widow of William H. Thomas, 81 IL Inf
Lawson N. Taylor, 3 MO State Militia Cav

Nancy Zoll widow of Upton Zoll, 94 Ohio Inf
David K. Speegle (Speesle), 1 Ala Cav
Mary Pearson, widow of Richard Pearson, 136 IL Inf

WASHINGTON COUNTY MISSOURI

The following abbreviations are used on the census: MO for Missouri, KY for Kentucky, NY for New York, NJ for New Jersey, PA and Penn for Pennsylvania, Tenn for Tennessee, Ark for Arkansas, Kan for Kansas, IL for Illinois, IN for Indiana, WVa for West Virginia, VA for Virginia, Wis and Wisc for Wisconsin, and Mich for Michigan, Inf for infantry, Cav for cavalry, Lt for light, Art for artillery, Vol for volunteer, Col for colored, reg for regiment.

NAME/UNIT

Virginia, widow of Sloman Wisdom, 29 MO Cav
Seyforth, Charles O., Sailor, El_fin
Forrester, Selatial, 31 MO Cav
White, Isom, 50 MO Inf
Doroney, Charles, 31 MO Inf
Conoway, Irwin, 50 MO Inf
Devine, Leander, 31 MO Inf
Hingston (Kingston), John. 62 US Col Inf
Parmelez, Robert, 31 MO Inf
Lyon, Riter, 31 MO Inf
Dunklin, Margaret widow of Samuel Dunklin, 2 MO Inf
Clay, Gabe, 56 US Col Inf
Pollitte, August, 35 MO Inf
Pollitte, Michael, 26 MO Inf
Myers, John, 50 MO Inf
Patterson, John P., 6 MO Inf
Henson, James A., 1 MO Lt. Inf
Pucket, James A., 50 MO Inf
Compton, George W., 30 MO Inf
Ramo, Robert, 50 MO Inf
Urban, John, 103 Ohio Inf
Shields, James A., 12 MO State Militia Cav
Eddleman, John R., 47 MO Inf
Bean, Andrew, 50 MO Inf
Glore, Robert T., 50 MO Inf
Williams, William, 16 KY
Harmoey, John E., 12 MO Cav
Gillan, Burwell, 8 MO Cav
Bell, John B., 13 MO Inf
Lister, Thomas, 62 US Inf
Deggendort, Joseph, 6 MO Inf
McCoy, Lewis B., 12 MO Cav, 13 MO Cav
Ellis, John I., 17 IL Inf
Ellis, Charles W., 133 IL Inf
Jolly, John, 31 MO Inf
Hunter, William T., 3 Missouri State Militia Cav
Perry, William M., 1 MO Lt. Art
Wall, David V., 47 MO Inf

Lachance, Joseph, 35 MO Inf
Hanbey, David S., 11 MO Inf
Miller, James, 31 MO Inf
Govro, Joseph R., 1 MO Art
Gray, John, 68 MO Cav
Olney, Orin D., 19 US Inf
William N. Rogers, 31 MO Inf
Valintine Frashel, 31 MO Inf
Eins Armstrong, 25 NJ Inf
Elias Helvey, 71 Ohio Inf
James Greenlee, 15 MO Inf
John W. Dawson, blacksmith, 5 IN Cav
Thomas Meyes, 90 PA Inf
Waymio Trakey widow of Joseph Trakey 30 MO Inf
Frank Govs, 22 Ohio Inf
John Borron, 22 Ohio Inf
Albert O. Glore, 4 Missouri State Militia Inf
Oe_ir Williams widow of George Williams, 57 PA Inf
Angeline Vaughn widow of _inett Vaughn, 67

Charles Reel, No Unit Given
Frank Lemon, 50 MO Inf
Frank Bone, 31 MO Inf
Mary Wishan widow of Jordan Wishon, No Unit Given
Wyatt M. Johnson, 149 IN Inf
Moses Cook, 67 MO Inf
Joseph Earlocker, 9 IL Cav
Levi Heeter, 42 IN Inf
William Dinsmore, 10 MO Cav
David M. Helms, 50 MO Inf
Wm. H. Evans, 31 MO Inf
William Miller, 5 IL Cav
Hea_lgrove Culton, 22 MO Inf
Oliver F. Beale, 6 MO Inf
Lewis D. Bone, 15 MO Inf
Annie Bloom widow of Faede__ Bloom, 22 Ohio Inf
Samuel R. McClay, 31 MO Inf
Edward Hamford, 55 MO Inf

Gabriel Borson, 35 MO Inf
Charles Strough, No Unit Given
William N. Potter, 15 MO Cav
John Evans, No Unit Given
Luke Huddleston, No Unit Given
Joseph Reese, No Unit Given
John G. W. Hormon, 47 MO Inf
William Keithcart, 50 MO Inf
George Fuchs, 2 MO Inf
Peter Cater alias Peter Smith, 65 MO Inf
John Fisher, 54 IN Inf
John Teado, 15 IL Inf
John Middleton, No Unit Given
John R. Hysins, No Unit Given
Thomas Eifos___, No Unit Given
Alman Daniel, 79 IL Inf
C. L. Boy___, No Unit Given
John Horn, No Unit Given
John N. Helms, 8_____
Jeremiah Postelwait, 17 WVa Inf
Winnie A. Thompson widow of Wm. Thompson, No Unit Given
James K. Northan____, MO Inf
Mary Chappel formerly widow of Edward Maul, 5 MO Inf
John W. Steele, 9 MO Inf
Patrick McCarron, 3 MO Cav
Charles McCarron, 6 MO Inf
Americus T. Shepherd, 2 MO Inf
John Jamison, 32 MO Inf
David L. Horton, 8 MO Cav
Thomas B. Self, 31 MO Vol Inf
John Fatchett, No Unit Given
Sarah A. West widow of George W. West, No Unit Given
Erving T. Jordan, No Unit Given
Richard Adams, 176 PA Inf
Thomas L. Simpson, 6 MO Inf
George W. Tate, 2 WVa Cav
Henry C. Thompson, No Unit Given
Johnathan Wishan, 91 Ohio Inf
Benj. F. Swacker, 51 VA Inf
Calvin F. Linzu__, No Unit Given
Robert F. Thompson, No Unit Given
Elbert S. Thompson, No Unit Given
Thomas N. Conway, 31 MO Inf
Charles F. Kine, 47 MO Inf
George Baker, Pvt. Essex
John Fo__hee, No Unit Given
Frank Westtom, 8 MO Inf
Mary G. Edgar widow of James Edgar, No Unit given
Andrew Wood, Confederate, No Unit Given
Mourice Prior, Confederate, No Unit Given
John M. Hughes, 50 MO Inf
Wm. T. Robinson, 32 MO Inf

George W. Woolford, 3 MO Cav
Miller Taylor, Confederate, 12 Tenn Cav
Thomas Elmore, Hones' Bat
John B. Means, 6 MO Inf
Francis M. Anderson, No Unit Given
Isaac E. Smith, No Unit Given
George R. McFarland, 15 MO Inf
Wm. _. Loomis, 3 Wis Inf
Jemima E. Wood widow of Andrew J. Wood, No Unit Given
Amos Crossman, 3 MO Cav
John A. Mills, 50 MO Inf
Stephen Denton, 32 MO Inf
Wm. L. Rice, East Missouri Militia
Edward H. Rice, 50 MO Inf
Joseph I. Robinson, 8 MO Inf
Reuben M. Hughes, 5 MO Inf
Joel K. P. Wood, 47 MO Inf
Robert f. Sutton, 5 MO Inf
John W. Bogarth, Sol US
John H. Bose, Sol US
Margaret L. Taylor widow SOL US
Grenville M. Coleman, Sol US
Mary C. Wigger, widow Sol US
John Beck, 7 Iowa Cav
Benjamin F. Johnson, 14 IL Inf
Louis Queen, 53 Ohio Inf
Robert D. Babel, 75 Ohio Inf
Nicholas Sohn, 3 KY Inf, Seaman Ram Lafayette Mississippi Squadron
Harmon Beakman, 10 MO Cav
Robert H. Moore, 50 MO Inf
Charles Akers, 3 MO Cav
Anderson Gann, 32 MO Cav
William W. Horusey, 3 MO Cav
Smith G. Breakenridge, 32 MO Cav
Nathan Davis, US
James W. S. Bayer, US
Christopher Hasque, US
Augusten K. Vivian, US
Da___ W. Smith, US
William Bogue, US
Harrison Inern, US
Angaline Henry, Soldier's widow
Hezekiah Inern –crossed out with no indication of whether Confederate
Dr. N. A. Bowern, 55 PA Inf
Constant Hudson, 11 MO Inf
James Napoleon Maxwell, 8 Ark Inf
Elijah Glover, 11 MO inf
Thomas G. Yarborough, 2 MO Cav
John James Roderick, 31 MO Inf
Richard H. Jackson, 31 MO Inf
Elias Hopkins, 14 MO Cav
William T. Wise, 21 MO Inf

Souson widow of George W. Northcutt, 31 MO Inf
Josiah Srauster, 131 PA Inf
David McEwing, 8 IL Inf
William G. Turnball, Sol US
John Burlbow, Sol US
Henderson, Thomas H., 3 Missouri State Militia Cav
Adams, Nelson, 18 MO Inf
Parker, John, 2 Missouri State Militia Cav
Halfiel, John, 9 IL Inf
Boning, Robert, 40 MO Inf
Asher, John, 1 Ark Inf
Maxwell, Thomas W., 50 MO Inf
Bryan, Bennet, 33 MO Inf
Bryan, Levie, 50 MO Inf
Bryan, Andrew F., 50 MO Inf
Hutchings, Harvey S., 33 MO Inf
McGrew, William B., 27 IN Inf
Adams, Daniel, 3 Missouri State Militia Cav
Adams, Francis M., 3 Missouri State Militia Cav
Bryan, Robert C., 33 MO Inf
Hardin, Joseph C., 10 Tenn Inf
Owens, John S., 2nd class fireman, NO 152, Gunboat Chil____
Turner, Richard T., 31 MO Inf
Strother, George A., 50 MO Inf
Lucinda Pope formerly widow of John R. Mann, 109 IL Inf
Marion, Priscilla D. widow of Marion, Leander G., 33 MO Inf
Ives, Thomas N., 48 MO Inf
Fortune, Jonathan, 3 Missouri State Militia Cav
Adams, John J., 32 MO Inf
Buckhart, Phillip, 11 PA Inf
Barger, Jacob S., 32 MO Inf
Bennett, James F., 3 Col Inf, 2 Col Cav
Gafer, Allen F., 31 MO Inf
Kirkpatrick, Margaret J. widow of Da___ W. Kirkpatrick, 21 MO Inf
Barger (Banger), William S., 50 MO Inf
Hide, John H. 50 MO Inf
Hatredge, Jessee, 47 MO Inf
Chadbourne, Lewis, 47 MO Inf
Adams, Zenas, 3 Missouri State Militia Cav
Dane, Littleton B., 13 KY Cav
Relfe, Lu___, 50 MO Inf
Larmer, James, 8 IL Inf
Fortune, Stephen L., 3 Missouri State Militia Cav
Tedder, William E., 3 Missouri State Militia Cav
Maxwell, Thomas A., 21 MO Inf
Farmer, Sarah L. former widow of Tedder, John W., 50 MO Inf
Francis M. Adams, No Unit Given
Mary A. Smith formerly Mary A. Wigger, No Unit Given
Thos. L. Judd, 13 Mich vol
Michael Thomas, No Unit Given
Barnabas Thomas, 5 IL Cav
Loss Hill, No Unit Given
John Hatfield, 9 IL Inf
J.P. Dunlop, No Unit Given
Frank Jenkins, 3 MO Cav
Jas G. B. Rasneck_, 32 MO Inf
J.F. Henslee, 50 MO Inf
Jno. Pyatt, 48 MO Inf
Danl Martin 48 VA Inf
Jane Midgett widow of James Midgett, No Unit Given
Jno. W. Flowers, No Unit Given
Jacob F. Cover, 14 IL Cav
James Abney, 1 KY Cav
Albert Gilliam, 15 MO Cav
Erma Turner wife of Brad Turner, 5 MO Cav
Geo. F. Mason, 38 MO Inf
Wm. Caringer, No Unit Given
Henry B. Cover, 29 IL Inf
James Duncan, 33 MO Inf
John Wilkerson, 33 MO Inf
William Wilkinson, 5 MO Inf
Henry C. Compton, Ohio
Isom Cashe, 18 MO Inf
Wood, Paris E., 144 IN Inf
Margaret E. widow of Samuel O. Stafiles, 31 MO Inf
Nethington, Henry W., 31 MO Inf
Gregory, Winfield S., 50 MO Inf
Martin, Robert R., 63 MO Inf
Jinkerson, Geo. W., 32 MO Inf, East Missouri Militia
Whitby, Joseph, 32 MO Inf, East Missouri Miitia
Harvey, Isaac L., 18 MO Inf
Sarah E. widow of William P. Edgar, 10 MO Cav
League, Wm. S., 50 MO Inf
Stevens, A. F., 12 MO State Militia Cav
Ion, Wm. C., 2 MO Cav, Merrill's Horse
White, Wm. M., 3 MO Cav
Wilson, Silas H., 32 MO Inf
Wilson, Jessey, 1 MO Art
Oakmull, Wm. A., 47 MO Inf
Nelson, George H., 45 MO Inf
Diens, Hugh L., 50 MO Inf
Eye, Laban, 11 MO Inf
Smith, Michael, 31 MO Inf
Matthews, Jonas, 68 MO Inf
Smith, Isaac, 23 Iowa Inf
Frederich Sansocie alias Fred Battice, 6 MO Cav
Edward Murphy alias Edward Jamison, 3 MO
Lanham, Childers W., 6 MO Cav

Mary Sansocie widow of Edward Sansocie, No Unit Given
Page, Joseph T., 22 Ohio Inf
Ogee, John, 6 MO
Patrney, John, 29 MO
Horine, Francis M. alias Frank Schultz, 3 MO Inf, 6 MO Cav
Jane Fallet widow of Charles A. Fallet, 22 Ohio Inf
Corden, Celestine, 11 MO Inf
Cook, James H., 32 MO Inf
Charboneau, William, 50 MO Inf
Evans, Thomas J., 2 MO Cav
Sparks, Alexander, 16 MO Cav
Rose, Christopher, 12 Kan Inf
Baugher, Eugene C., 11 MO Inf, 10 MO Inf, 13 MO Inf
Arconce Sansocie widow of Louis Sansocie, 32 MO Inf
Amalie, Joseph B., 6 MO Cav
Yarbraugh, Owen, 2 MO cav
Hulsey, Harrelson G., 2 MO Cav
Cook, James, 32 MO Inf
Courtain, Francois, 26 MO Inf
Louis Amlie alias Louis Hamlin, 26 MO Inf
Courtain, Bontemas, 15 MO Inf
Elizabeth Coleman formerly widow of John Thebeau, No Unit Given
Smith, George W., 5 MO Inf
Bowers, Reubon, 16 US Inf
Rutledge, John R., 3 MO Cav
Jackson, Jasper, No Unit Given
Ward, Michael, 31 MO Inf
Mary Leasy widow of Daniel Casey No Unit Given
Matilda Lewis former widow of George W. Wise, No Unit Given
Joshie Rulo fomer widow of Courlois, Felix, 35 MO Inf
Courlois, John, No Unit Given
Charfell, Charles, No Unit Given
John Crum, 150 IL Inf
Forkline Wiley, Confederate, 44 Tenn Inf
Becky Oharver widow of Henry Oharver, 10 MO Cav
Boone Bryan, 31 MO Inf
Henry Gunther, 153 __ Inf
Theodore Courtois, 15 MO Inf
Xaviar Politte, 26 MO Inf
Francis X. Omly, 26 MO Inf
Antoine Merceille, 29 MO Inf
Anthony Declous, 31 MO Inf
Henry Pratt, 35 MO Inf
John Sansocie, 35 MO Inf
Felix Boyer, 50 MO Inf
Dizly Ackison widow of John M. Ackison, 25 MO Inf
Josephine Sauers widow of Joseph Sauers, 47 MO Inf
Nancy Off widow of Francis Off, No Unit Given
Abraham Politte, 29 MO Inf
Joseph Politte, 26 MO Inf
Henry St. Mary, Mexican War Veteran
Frank Courtois, 29 MO Inf
Antoine Mesey, 35 MO Inf
John Politte, 35 MO Inf
Joseph T. Boyer, 1 Nebraska Inf
Charles Sansocie, 5 MO Inf
John W. Martin, 6 MO Inf
James M. White, Confederate, 2 MO Inf
Lester Henry, Confederate, Reeves Reg, MC Crays Brigade
Joseph Cane, 6 MO Cav
Agile Merceille widow of US Sol
Daniel Abbey, Sol US
Richard Brimm, 50 M Inf
James Juellerat, 31 MO Inf
Mary Theotick Boyer widow of Frederick Boyer, 15 MO Inf
William H. Stuart, No Unit Given
Christopher C. Hays, 3 MO Cav
Antoine Troker, 35 MO Inf
Thomas Dean, 32 MO Inf
Charles Sullivan, 35 MO Inf
Tojuile Boursow, 35 MO Inf
Francis Bequette, 15 MO Inf
Eli Barger, 35 MO Inf
Adaline O. Colerman widow of Severin Boyer, 35 MO Inf
Alexius Coleman, 15 MO Inf
Zeno Boyer, 35 MO Inf
Simon Boyer, 1 Nebraska Cav
John T. Thebeau, 35 MO Inf
Maida Politte, 35 MO Inf
David Boyer, 35 MO Inf
Aug. Norton, 3 NY Cav
Elisha Boyer, 50 MO Inf
Bagg, David, 5 IL Cav
Hartzell, Silas, MO Home Guard
Christopher, Robert, 1 MO Inf
Hanson, Joseph B., 7 Kan Cav
Boyer, John, 50 MO Inf
Boyer, Furman, 31 MO Inf, 32 MO Inf
Rosene widow of Sefroid Parel, 1 Missouri State Militia Inf
Lachance, Mary widow of John Lachance, 31 MO Inf
Crawford, William, No Unit Given
Jarrett, William, 31 MO Inf
Reando, Antoine, No Unit Given
Richardson, William, 31 MO Inf

Wilkinson, John L., 7 Iowa Inf
Bourchard, Mathew, 31 MO Inf
Boyer, Jacob, 35 MO Inf
Paul, Thos. H. B., 31 MO Inf
Boyer, Felix, 31 MO Inf
Goff, William M., 50 MO Inf
Politte, Neree, 15 MO Inf
Willson, Asberry, 38 IL Inf
Lake, Luman C., 3 Wisc Inf
Richeson, John O., 26 MO Inf
Golden, Daniel, 6 MO Inf
McAtee, George, 149 IL Inf
Major , Charles H., says lost discharge
Oster, Daniel, 15 MO Inf
Duclas, John F., 15 MO Inf
Melinda A. wide of Elisha J. Puckett, 13 MO Inf
Nicholas Lachance, 35 MO Inf
Zarmma, Maure, 5 US Inf
Duclas, John, 5 US Inf
Winstead, William, 4 MO Inf
Morris, Jeremiah, 50 MO Inf
Guyer, Michael, 22 Ohio Inf
Hiram Whiteside, US Sol
Jeremia Morris, US Sol (could be duplicate entry)
Michael Guyer, US Soldier (could be duplicate entry)

WAYNE COUNTY MISSOURI

The following abbreviations were used on the census: MO for Missouri, IL for Illinois, IN for Indiana, NJ for New Jersey, NY for New York, Pa or Penn for Pennsylvania, Tenn for Tennessee, KY for Kentucky, Kan for Kansas, Ark for Arkansas, Mich for Michigan, Wis for Wisconsin, CT for Connecticut, NC for North Carolina, Ala for Alabama, Inf for infantry, Cav for cavalry, Lt for light, art for artillery, vol for volunteer, USS for United States Soldier, Col for colored, Reg for regiment, Vet for veteran, res for reserve, and Tel for Telegraph.

NAME/UNIT

Barnett, James W., No Unit Given
Bates, George, 116 Ohio Inf
Mary A. widow of Francis M. Bunyard, 47 MO Inf
Leitinger, Anthony, No Unit Given
Nevins, Charles W., 41 IL Inf, 8 IL Inf
Brown, Marion J., 10 IL Inf.
Reed, Samuel B., 1 MO Inf
Stokeley, William, 47 MO Inf
Conline, James, 29 IL Inf
Short, John, 14 IL Cav
Sweet, Sterling, 11 NY Cav
Hartley, John A., 115 PA Inf
Harrison, Bengerman F., 29 MO Inf
McGuire, James M., 1 Iowa Cav
Hayley, Charles, 42 IL Inf, 17 IL Cav
Storrs, Douglas M., 16 Ohio Inf
Scott, Charles W., 72 IL Inf
Westmoreland, Robert, 5 KY Cav
Whitman, Conrade S., 48 IL
Malloy, John T., 31 MO Inf
Anderson, James A., 2 Ark Cav
Kent, William, 13 KY Cav
Wakefield, Thomas, 46 IL Inf
Wilson, James H., 13 IL Cav
Long, Francis M., 117 IL Inf
Gilbreath, Isaac C., 29 MO Inf
Krimminger, J. C., 50 MO Inf
Mosley, Andrew, 154 IL Inf
Church, Andrew, 50 MO Inf
Pittman, James, 5 Tenn Cav
Dawson, Moses P., 53 Ohio Inf
Warnock, F.M., 47 MO Inf
Eddington, Jas. A., 47 MO Inf
Schiek, John, 45 NY Inf
Robert Alcorn, US Sol
Richard Lee, US Sol
Ann E. Gilbreth, widow US Sol
Austin Groves, US Sol
William Nossett, US Sol
Jesse Hall, US Sol
Chas. G. Scott, US Sol
Martha A. Mulikin, widow US Sol
Joseph Short, US Sol
Peter Weber, US Sol
Jas T. Smith, US Sol
Frances E. _andall, widow US Sol
Jerome B. Shular, US Sol
Della _. Belinan, widow US Sol
Thomas Tolin, 17 IL Inf
Thomas Philips, 4 KY Cav
Jonathan Dees, 7 Kan Cav
David Manning, 3 MO Cav
Susan Ann widow of Steven Canterberry, 40 MO Inf
George Owens, 18 IL Inf
Richard W. Alexander, 47 MO Inf
Harvey Biggerstaff, 3 MO Cav
Nancy widow of James Elliot, No Unit Given
Ivenson M. Ward, 68 MO Cav
William C. Wood, 32 MO Inf
Thomas Myers, MO Cav
Adam Terry, 130 IN Inf
David Rains, 6 MO Cav
William P. Hillen, 3 MO Cav
Mary J. widow of John F. Manning, 144 IL Inf
Collins W. Cutler, 9 Mich Cav
Joseph Langley, 6 MO Cav
Maggie L. Breath widow of John E. Breath, 144 IL Inf
John R. Nibby, 176 Ohio Inf
Charles T. Howard, 2 Wis Cav
John Satterly, 16 Wis Inf
John M. Hunt, 61 IL Inf
Curr_e A. Creath, 1 Col Cav
Benjaman Oliver, 15 CT Inf
Mary widow of Benedict Grandl (Grande), No Unit Given
Charles Fingads, 31 MO Inf
Thomas Millard, 30 Ohio Inf
William C. Carter, 33 MO Inf
Edward Letts, 18 Ohio Cav

Elisha T. England, 47 MO Inf
Harmon Sparlany, 59 IN Inf
Detric Sonnamakiar, 13 IL Cav
Ella Goff former widow of Franklin Fignny (Fanny), 29 MO Inf
William Thursland, 28 IN Inf
John C. Bonny, No Unit Given
Urius Nichols, 16 PA Inf, 87 PA Inf
Harry Clark, No Unit Given
Thomas Mansfield, 47 MO Inf
Jefferson C. Davis, No Unit Given
Eastner C. widow of Manturo P_gg, 47 MO Inf
Franklin Forsull, 47 MO Inf
Martha A. widow of Andrew _. Duncan, 47 MO inf
Saphronia widow of Joseph Steel, 47 MO Inf
George Warnock, 47 MO Inf
Joel H. Myers, No Unit Given
Gram C. Hockwirth, 47 MO Inf
Thomas Downs, No Unit Given
Henry Fry, 40 MO Inf
John Eads, 3 NC Inf
Catharine widow of David L. Koons, Ohio Inf
Marius Hallerbrand, 47 MO Inf
Thomas A. Duffield, 2 Col Cav
William T. Leepe, 12 Missouri State Militia Cavalry, 3 Missouri State Militia Cavalry
M.P. Page, 47 MO Inf
Joseph D. Wallis, 47 MO Inf
Nathan Chamberlin, MO Militia
John N. Carmahure, Sol US
Christian F. Sopper, Sol US
John R. Gring, Sol US
John Ross, Sol US
Clark Mann, Sol US
Eliza B. Igurmis, widow Sol US
Sophriama Steele widow US Sol
Jasper N. Chatman, 31 MO Inf, 32 Moinf
Jasper M. Standley, 5 MO Cav
Joseph Atwell, IL
Peter S. Welch, 3 IN Cav
Joseph Strictland, 20 IN Inf
Henry _. Mabrey, 3 MO Cav, 31 MO Inf
Jacoson Inman, 24 MO inf
Samuel D. Milam, 25 IN
Thomas Terne alias Thomas Tune, No Unit Given
Willis W. Slaris, 29 MO Inf
James R. Matery, 31 MO Inf
Nancy J. Club widow of James Ragsdale, 76 MO Inf
Stephen Whitt, 24 MO Inf
Stehpen A. Whit, 47 MO Inf (could be same person as above in a second unit)
Andrew J. Hicks, 49 IL Inf
Oliver P. Woodruff, 33 MO Inf

Joel L. Morgan, 1 KY Cav
William J. Mathews, 60 IL Inf
William H. Morgan, 47 MO inf
Daniel Moore, 3 MO Cav, 15 MO Cav
William Hasting, 8 MO Cav
W. T. Vincent, 5 KY Cav
Daniel Colson, 36 Ohio Inf
Joshua Pigg, 8 Tenn Cav
Maison Wilson, 3 MO Cav
John B. Derr alias John B. Durrow, 16 KY Cav
Joel M. Taylor, 97 IL Inf
Marthey Wartman widow of __nnial C. Faulkner, 44 IL Inf
Parick J. Srelly, Seaman, Farragut's Squadron
William Cheeseman alias William Chessman, 89 IL Inf, 59 IL Inf
Joseph B. Deaton, Sol US
John R. Potter, Sol US
Francis M. Shipton, Sol US
B. Jos. T. Bell, Sol US
Dadamra Walker, widow US Sol
J.M. Smith, Confederate, No Unit Given
White, D. J., 7 Virg. Cav
White, S. E. late widow of G. W. Hall, 44 IN Inf
Underwood, J., 50 MO Inf
Nelson, James, 62 IL Inf
Young, J.B., 47 MO Inf
Jobe Stilts, Sol US
Berry, William, 12 Missouri State Militia Cavalry
Bounds, J.M., 47 MO Inf
Frederick, Wm. R., 64 MO Inf
Long, S.B., 12 Missouri State Militia Cavalry, 5 Missouri State Militia Cavalry
Davis, T. R., 31 MO Inf
Neighbors, J. W., MO
White, Alex, 31 MO
McCalaster, James, Confederate, 31 MO Inf
Ward, Yancy, Confederate, 44 NC Inf
Davis, John A., 31 MO Inf
Pruitt, Nathan, Confederate, 34 NC Inf
Johns, Felix, 3 MO, 14 MO
Susan Hill widow of L. D. Hill, 3 MO Inf
Sutherland, J.P., 47 MO Inf, 12 Missouri State Militia
Schall, D. F., 123 Ohio Inf
Scritchfield, J., 3 MO Cav
Moore, J. L., Confederate, 3 KY Mtd. Inf
Butler, G. W., Confederate, White's Cav
Butler, S. widow of H. Sanley, Confederate, 31 MO Cav
Estes, Noel, 47 MO Cav
Powers, P. L., 47 MO Inf
Kelley, late widow of S. R. Kelley, 3 MO Inf
Lawhorn, L.C. widow of D. S. Kelley, 27 Ohio Inf

Underwood, W. R., 12 Missouri State Militia
Ware, John, 119 IL Inf
Jines, Alex, (US) 11 KY Inf
May, Wm. A. (US) 97 IN Inf
Wilfong, J. W. Confederate, 47 MO Cav (?)
Fry, T.H., (US) 12 MO cav
Fry, M.A, widow of Higgines, John (US), 25 Reg. Inf
Brown, J. A. (US), 10 Iowa Cav
Conrad, S. P. (US), 50 MO Inf
Anderson, S. P. Confederate, did not know
Hadock, T. J., (US), 58 IN Inf
Stilts, Peter, 2 MO Cav
McGee, Agnes late widow of Daniel McGee, Confederate, No Unit Given
Kenaday, S. A. widow of Wm. Kenaday Confederate, No Unit Given
Coots, A. J., 47 MO Cav
Simpkins, John, 29 IN Inf
Cado, Richard, Confederate, 2 MO Cav
Phiveata Payne late widow of Lovell Fulk, 43 IN Inf
Kick, Jacob, (US), 7 KY Cav
Davis, Joseph, 120 IL Inf
Robert Hood, 67 IN Inf
John W. Lockell, 8 Missouri State Militia
Nancy J. widow of Ownbey, Andrew L., 47 MO, 39 MO Inf
Francis M. widow of Alford B. Allen, 47 MO Inf
Casander widow of Murhpey White, 47 MO Inf
William L. Ward, 47 MO Inf
McClanahan, Christofer C., Confederate, 27 Tenn Inf
Ward, Melger M., 8 MO Cav
Huffman, Henry A. ----lined out with no indication of Confederate
Collier, Drury, 47 MO Inf
Huffman, Henry A., 58 Georgia Inf (probably the above lined out entry)
William R. Ward, 8 MO Cav
Polser Ward, 47 MO Inf
Charles P. Ward, 47 MO Inf
Julias A. Ward, MO Cav
Crammier C. Price, 13 MO Cav
Henry Hogon, Confederate, 23 Tenn Inf
John E. Ward, Confederate, MO Inf
Miles Tompson, 47 MO Cav
Preneus Hovies, Confederate, Cav
Ensebius Hovies, 47 MO Inf
Alford P. Crump, 56 MO Inf
Walter M. Bell, Unknown
Jerone B. Barnkart, Confederate, MO Inf
Tomas U. School, Confederate, MO Inf
Falima F. Dixon widow of Tomas B. Dickson, Unknown
Henry Barks, 5 Missouri State Militia Cav
Thomas Costphen, 47 MO Inf
Thomas Crites, 2 MO Cav
Peter Shuler, Confederate, Unknown
James Grisham, 3 MO Cav
Joseph Overheels, 134 Ohio
Louiza M. widow of Miles Hefner Confederate, Unknown
Wilford Abernathy, 3 MO Cav
Joseph Swasford, 6 IL Cav
William S. Gaines, Surgeon, 95 Ohio Inf
Clayborne Barnes, Confederate, 28 Tenn Inf
Danel Barks, 50 MO If
John E. Parker, Confederate, 12 MO Cav
John R. Simpson, Confederate, 2 KY Cav
Henry Fronabarger, Confederate, Unknown
Leeman Guthrie, 1 Ala Cav
Mike L. Butts, 47 MO Inf
Francis E. Whitemer, 47 MO Inf
Fled J. F. Moser, 3 MO Cav
ohe Skaggs, 47 MO Inf
Wm. W. Darnell, 47 MO Inf
Joseph East, 50 MO Inf
Jas. H. Willmore, 1 Tenn Inf
Joseph Dimond, 149 IL Inf
Carlis Greer, 130 IL Inf
Chas. B. Wakefield, 47 MO Inf
Jas. H. Kuze, 3 IL Cav
Sympson C. Sutton, 47 MO Inf
John L. Bennett, 47 MO Inf
John W. Evans, 47 MO Inf
George W. Revis, 49 KY Inf
Hasio S. Winter, 56 IL Inf
John L. Skeaner, 47 MO Inf
John M. Dement, 4 Ark Cav
Jas. H. Jhgnes, 4 MO Cav
John Croley, 47 MO Inf
Hy S. Good, 47 MO Inf
Thomas H. Snyder, 6 MO Inf
Henry Hunter, 9 KY Inf
Wm. P. White, 31 MO Inf
Frank M. Parker, 47 MO Inf
James C. Paullus, 47 MO Inf
Abecagy Dorsey, 47 MO Inf
Jas S. Johns, 32 MO Inf
Thomas Spurgeon, 8 Tenn Inf
John H. Williamson, 68 East Missouri Militia Inf
John B. Willmore, 47 MO Inf
Rebecca Bess widow of Absalum Bess, 47 MO Inf
Lemis H. Linville, 68 East Missouri Militia Inf
Wm. F. Taylor, 47 MO Inf
James V. Gregory, 47 MO Inf
C. F. Benita__, 50 MO Inf
Joseph A. Bennett, 47 MO Inf
James Landon, Sol US
Geo. W. Luttrell, Sol US

Sarah C. widow of Willie C. Thornburg, Postage Clerk Ramplate
Jerrymiah J. Rose, 61 IL Cav
John A. Pitrup, 47 MO Inf
Joel Westmoreland, 12 KY Inf
Harrison Westmoreland, 12 KY Inf
William H. Lawson, 10 MO Inf, 11 MO Inf
Robart Moore, 3 MO Cav
Winfield Praul, 154 IL Inf
James Walker, 17 Iowa Inf
Robert Cassaday, 148 Penn Inf
John M. Dale, 31 MO Inf
John C. Croy (Gray), 47 MO Inf
Jesse Westmoreland, 12 KY Inf
James M. Birdwell, 1 Ark Inf
Victor M. Preslin, 1 MO Lt. Art
Damon J. Taylor, 47 MO Inf
Martha J. Pipkin widow of John Pipkin, 47 MO Inf
Timothy P. Baird, 31 MO Inf
Elgin Dunegan, 8 MO Inf, 3 MO Cav
Jacob Hildebidal, 80 IL Inf
M. _. Warren, 47 MO Inf
Thomas C. Mccorkle, 97 IL Inf
Horatio T. Fulton, 47 MO Inf
Samuel J. Brunebow, 47 MO Inf
Annie C. Morgan former widow of William C. Croy (Gray), 47 MO Inf
James Davis, 47 MO Inf
Thomas G. Berryman, 3 MO Cav
C. R. McCormick, 47 MO Inf
Samuel Max, 11 Ohio Inf
Loueasy J. Morgan widow of William L. Morgan, 47 MO Inf
H. C. Wilkinson, 47 MO Inf
Henry Shoemaker, 14 IN Inf
John H. Close, 126 IL Inf
Alive M. Williams widow of John Williams, 47 MO Inf
Annie widow of John Wallace, 3 MO Cav
William Atchison, 72 MO Cav
Samuel Vallance, 10 KY Cav
James H. Barker, 47 MO Inf
John F. Harmon, 6 Ohio Cav
Willie H. Keeland, 47 MO Inf
C. B. L. Rowland, 47 MO inf
Mary Henson, Soldier
Sabetha A. Harris, Soldier
Matilda Montgomery widow of Albert Montgomery, 39 MO
Golson Phelps, 11 KY, 35 KY Inf
Thomas A. Ward, 47 MO inf
Ruth E. Montgomery widow of Christopher G. Montgomery, Confederate, MO Cav
Green D. Barrett, Confederate, MO Cav
Josiah Payne, 68 MO Militia
Irwin D. Cooper, 24 MO Inf
_gustus Smith, 10 Vet Res
Thomas J. Collins, 50 IN Inf
James J. White, 47 MO Inf
Martha E. widow of Cagger, George, 38 IL Inf
Abner Bennett, 47 MO inf
Philip, H. H. Hickman, 4 MO Inf
___ham A. Kresmer (very faint) NO Unit Given
Mary H. _____ widow of Nicklas__, William _. 145 IL Inf
Miter B. Edwards, 7 Tenn Cav
Uriah S. Watkins, 12 NJ Vol
Glancer D. Ald___, 6 MO Cav
William R. Hubbard, 47 MO Inf
Wal____ H. Birmingham, 47 MO Inf
Joel, A. Meadows, 47 MO Inf
Edward P. Settle, 47 MO Inf
Richard E. Buehler, US Tel Staff
Jesse D. Pickard, 71 IN Inf
Lewis Gulley, 52 KY Inf
Chester Kirkpatrick, 32 MO Inf
E. Lesbery Park, 62 IL Cav, 6 IL Cav
Benjamin F. Montgomery, 47 MO Inf
James C. Creasy, 1 Tenn Inf
Samuel C. Carlton, 49 IL Inf
William B. Wilson, 47 MO Inf
James A. Kite, 12 MO Cav
Arthur F._____, 49 IL Inf
William E. Harrington, Soldier
Diana Green widow US Soldier
Hugh Walker, US Soldier
Thomas Giles, US Soldier
William Tridwell, USS
Eliza J. Donelson, widow USS
King A. Dover, USS
Martha A. Baunds, widow USS
Mariah Garison, widow USS
Reuben Bennett, USS
George Miller, USS
Thomas Lawson, USS
John Sweeze, USS
Willie Lupcy, USS

Other Heritage Books by Linda L. Green:

1890 Union Veterans Census: Special Enumeration Schedules Enumerating Union Veterans and Widows of the Civil War. Missouri Counties: Bollinger, Butler, Cape Girardeau, Carter, Dunklin, Iron, Madison, Mississippi, New Madrid, Oregon, Pemiscot, Petty, Reynolds, Ripley, St. Francois, St. Genevieve, Scott, Shannon, Stoddard, Washington, and Wayne

Alabama 1850 Agricultural and Manufacturing Census: Volume 1 for Dale, Dallas, Dekalb, Fayette, Franklin, Greene, Hancock, and Henry Counties

Alabama 1850 Agricultural and Manufacturing Census: Volume 2 for Jackson, Jefferson, Lawrence, Limestone, Lowndes, Macon, Madison, and Marengo Counties

Alabama 1850 Agricultural and Manufacturing Census: Volume 3 for Autauga, Baldwin, Barbour, Benton, Bibb, Blount, Butler, Chambers, Cherokee, Choctaw, Clarke, Coffee, Conecuh, Coosa, and Covington Counties

Alabama 1850 Agricultural and Manufacturing Census: Volume 4 for Marion, Marshall, Mobile, Monroe, Montgomery, Morgan, Perry, Pickens, Pike, Randolph, Russell, St. Clair, Shelby, Sumter, Talladega, Tallapoosa, Tuscaloosa, Walker, Washington, and Wilcox Counties

Alabama 1860 Agricultural and Manufacturing Census: Volume 1 for Dekalb, Fayette, Franklin, Greene, Henry, Jackson, Jefferson, Lawrence, Lauderdale, and Limestone Counties

Alabama 1860 Agricultural and Manufacturing Census: Volume 2 for Lowndes, Madison, Marengo, Marion, Marshall, Macon, Mobile, Montgomery, Monroe, and Morgan Counties

Alabama 1860 Agricultural and Manufacturing Census: Volume 3 for Autauga, Baldwin, Barbour, Bibb, Blount, Butler, Calhoun, Chambers, Cherokee, Choctaw, Clarke, Coffee, Conecuh, Coosa, Covington, Dale, and Dallas Counties

Alabama 1860 Agricultural and Manufacturing Census: Volume 4 for Perry, Pickens, Pike, Randolph, Russell, Shelby, St. Clair, Sumter, Tallapoosa, Talladega, Tuscaloosa, Walker, Washington, Wilcox, and Winston Counties

Delaware 1850–1860 Agricultural Census, Volume 1

Delaware 1870–1880 Agricultural Census, Volume 2

Delaware Mortality Schedules, 1850–1880; Delaware Insanity Schedule, 1880 Only

Dunklin County, Missouri Marriage Records: Volume 1, 1903–1916

Dunklin County, Missouri Marriage Records: Volume 2, 1916–1927

Florida 1850 Agricultural Census

Florida 1860 Agricultural Census

Georgia 1860 Agricultural Census: Volume 1 Comprises the Counties of Appling, Baker, Baldwin, Banks, Berrien, Bibb, Brooks, Bryan, Bullock, Burke, Butts, Calhoun, Camden, Campbell, Carroll, Cass, Catoosa, Chatham, Charlton, Chattahooche, Chattooga, and Cherokee

Georgia 1860 Agricultural Census: Volume 2 Comprises the Counties of Clark, Clay, Clayton, Clinch, Cobb, Colquitt, Coffee, Columbia, Coweta, Crawford, Dade, Dawson, Decatur, Dekalb, Dooly, Dougherty, Early, Echols, Effingham, Elbert, Emanuel, Fannin, and Fayette

Kentucky 1850 Agricultural Census for Letcher, Lewis, Lincoln, Livingston, Logan, McCracken, Madison, Marion, Marshall, Mason, Meade, Mercer, Monroe, Montgomery, Morgan, Muhlenburg, and Nelson Counties

Kentucky 1860 Agricultural Census: Volume 1 for Floyd, Franklin, Fulton, Gallatin, Garrard, Grant, Graves, Grayson, Green, Greenup, Hancock, Hardin, and Harlin Counties

Kentucky 1860 Agricultural Census: Volume 2 for Harrison, Hart, Henderson, Henry, Hickman, Hopkins, Jackson, Jefferson, Jessamine, Johnson, Morgan, Muhlenburg, Nelson, and Nicholas Counties

Kentucky 1860 Agricultural Census: Volume 3 for Kenton, Knox, Larue, Laurel, Lawrence, Letcher, Lewis, Lincoln, Livingston, Logan, Lyon, and Madison Counties

Kentucky 1860 Agricultural Census: Volume 4 for Mason, Marion, Magoffin, McCracken, McLean, Marshall, Meade, Mercer, Metcalfe, Monroe and Montgomery Counties

Louisiana 1860 Agricultural Census: Volume 1 Covers Parishes: Ascension, Assumption, Avoyelles, East Baton Rouge, West Baton Rouge, Boosier, Caddo, Calcasieu, Caldwell, Carroll, Catahoula, Clairborne, Concordia, Desoto, East Feliciana, West Feliciana, Franklin, Iberville, Jackson, Jefferson, Lafayette, Lafourche, Livingston, and Madison

Louisiana 1860 Agricultural Census: Volume 2

Maryland 1860 Agricultural Census: Volumes 1 and 2

Mississippi 1850 Agricultural Census: Volumes 1–3

Mississippi 1860 Agricultural Census: Volume 1 Comprises the Following Counties: Lowndes, Madison, Marion, Marshall, Monroe, Neshoba, Newton, Noxubee, Oktibbeha, Panola, Perry, Pike, and Pontotoc

Mississippi 1860 Agricultural Census: Volume 2 Comprises the Following Counties: Rankin, Scott, Simpson, Smith, Tallahatchie, Tippah, Tishomingo, Tunica, Warren, Wayne, Winston, Yalobusha, and Yazoo

Missouri 1850 Agricultural Census: Volumes 1–5

Montgomery County, Tennessee 1850 Agricultural Census

New Madrid County, Missouri Marriage Records, 1899–1924

North Carolina 1850 Agricultural Census: Volumes 1–4

Pemiscot County, Missouri Marriage Records, January 26, 1898 to September 20, 1912: Volume 1

Pemiscot County, Missouri Marriage Records, November 1, 1911 to December 6, 1922: Volume 2

South Carolina 1860 Agricultural Census: Volumes 1–3
Tennessee 1850 Agricultural Census: Volumes 1–5
Tennessee 1860 Agricultural Census: Volumes 1 and 2
Texas 1850 Agricultural Census, Volume 1: Anderson through Hunt Counties
Texas 1850 Agricultural Census, Volume 2: Jackson through Williamson Counties
Texas 1860 Agricultural Census, Volumes 1–5
Virginia 1850 Agricultural Census, Volumes 1–5
Virginia 1860 Agricultural Census, Volumes 1–4
West Virginia 1850 Agricultural Census, Volumes 1 and 2
West Virginia 1860 Agricultural Census, Volume 1–4

www.ingramcontent.com/pod-product-compliance
Lightning Source LLC
Chambersburg PA
CBHW081258170426
43198CB00017B/2837